CHRIS ADAMS

Can We Call You Part Time?

Innovating for the Future of Ministry

Copyright © 2022 by Chris Adams

All rights reserved. No part of this publication may be reproduced, stored or transmitted in any form or by any means, electronic, mechanical, photocopying, recording, scanning, or otherwise without written permission from the publisher. It is illegal to copy this book, post it to a website, or distribute it by any other means without permission.

Chris Adams has no responsibility for the persistence or accuracy of URLs for external or third-party Internet Websites referred to in this publication and does not guarantee that any content on such Websites is, or will remain, accurate or appropriate.

Designations used by companies to distinguish their products are often claimed as trademarks. All brand names and product names used in this book and on its cover are trade names, service marks, trademarks and registered trademarks of their respective owners. The publishers and the book are not associated with any product or vendor mentioned in this book. None of the companies referenced within the book have endorsed the book.

First edition

ISBN: 979-8-9863921-1-0

This book was professionally typeset on Reedsy. Find out more at reedsy.com

To the One that loved me even before I was born, to the church of Jesus Christ, and to the Spirit of God that shapes and animates everything!

I, the Lord of sea and sky
I have heard my people cry
All who dwell in dark and sin
My hand will save
I who made the stars of night
I will make their darkness bright
Who will bear my light to them?
Whom shall I send?

Here I am, Lord
Is it I, Lord?
I have heard You calling in the night
I will go, Lord
If You lead me
I will hold Your people in my heart

-Daniel L Schutte

Contents

I Part One

1 "I am never going to be anyone's pastor again!"   3
2 Crisis of Church Leadership Demands Change   11
3 Realistic Expectations for Small Church Growth   21
4 Laboring For The Gospel   30

II Part Two

5 Myth of the Full-Time Pastor: Hit and Hope   43
6 Part-Time Pastor Paul   57
7 Pastor John Calvin was Focused Local Theologian   68
8 Helpful and Not: Pastoral Gifts   77

III Part Three

9 You Can Do This!   95
10 What's It Look Like? Some Models for Ministry Leadership   103
11 Best Practices for Part-time ministry   112
12 Final Thoughts: Gifts of God for the People of God   130
13 Appendix   137

Epilogue	139
About the Author	143

Part One

The Time to Innovate is Now

1

"I am never going to be anyone's pastor again!"

"The human mind plans the way, but the Lord directs the steps."
–Proverbs 16:9

"I am never going to be anyone's pastor ever again!" That's what I told people when I left full-time ministry in October of 2017. That year was my twentieth year in ministry—twenty years filled with a combination of part-time and full-time work with both churches and non-profit organizations. I had served as a youth pastor, a Christian educator, a community liaison with an urban nonprofit, an associate pastor, and a head of staff for a large, multi-staffed congregation. But by 2017, I was ready to be done with all of it.

Many have used the word "burnout" to describe what I was experiencing. Over the years, I watched colleagues of mine in ministry go through such a season, a result of too much responsibility, too many hours, and not enough support from the congregation and other colleagues. I told myself, as they likely told themselves, that it would not happen to me. And so

I continued to serve, year after year, moving from position to position as my career grew.

In 2012, I moved with my family to Nashville, Tennessee to lead what I thought would be my dream job. The congregation was very socially active, theologically moderate, leaning progressive, and ready for new leadership. At least, that's what they told me, and I believed them. But they weren't as ready for change as they seemed to think they were, which made effective leadership and follower-ship very difficult.

In 2017, I was feeling a combination of burnout and frustration over a system of congregational ministry that set up the pastor and congregation for failure. It just didn't seem to work anymore. All the necessary change was assumed to be my work alone, along with the other professional staff, while the members of the congregation were struggling to come to grips with the changing reality of church and culture, their new ministry in response, and what if anything would be required them in this new reality. Everybody was frustrated and I was struggling to find my voice as a leader. At times I pushed too hard and then flipped to not caring enough to do much of anything. By the end, I was just tired and isolated.

In the interest of my emotional health I sensed it was time for a shift. Paula, my wife, had started a thriving real estate business in Nashville, which had become the new "it" city in America. She had been successful by every measure. What was more interesting to me was the interactions she had with her clients. Real estate agents sometimes know far more about the personal lives of their clients than any other profession, even more than a pastor. They know their bank account information, their job situation, their family dynamics, and their successes and failures. Real estate agents get involved with their clients at key moments in their lives, like marriage, birth of children, divorce, and death. If a pastor wanted to find a place to serve where the "harvest is plentiful and the workers are few,"[1] then I thought this might be the place. I wanted to be part of making a difference in people's lives like that. That's why I went into the ministry in the first place—to change and transform lives.

So, I resigned my position vowing to never look back. After all, I said, twenty years is long enough to serve. I had many friends from my alma mater, The Citadel, the Military College of South Carolina, who at the time were retiring after serving our nation's military for twenty years. "That's what I did," I told myself, "I served my time and now it's time for something else." Friends and colleagues from that time in my life would tell you I was resolved. I can almost hear myself patting myself on the back, all done!

A little smile comes to my face though when I think back on those days now. Most people know the quote from Woody Allen, "If you want to make God laugh, tell him your plans." Not as many people know the quote is based on a Yiddish Proverb: *We plan. God laughs.* The point is, we never know what God has in mind for us. And sometimes, if we did know, we wouldn't be willing to accept it.

I studied online and tested for my real estate license at the end of 2017. Before long, I started working alongside my wife in our business. I became Rev. Dr. Chris Adams, Realtor. Paula is the kind of person that builds confidence and trust, one person at a time, one home at a time, over and over again, until one day a very successful business has been built. Our clients count on us to help them with every aspect of real estate. Buying new

---

[1] Luke 10:2 (NRSV)

homes, selling existing ones, investment properties, advice on the market, and building personal wealth are all things we help our clients navigate every day. Eighty percent of our business comes from referrals from clients we have already worked with. We are a part of people's lives in profound and meaningful ways. What a blessing for me it has been to have another career just waiting for me to step into. I don't take that lightly, and routinely give thanks to God. In fact, I give thanks to God several times a day. Every time I compose an email, it always ends with one word: Grateful!

Maybe it was that sense of gratitude that manifested a desire to serve again, because by the end of 2018 I was entertaining some new ideas about ministry. What if I just started to preach again, just a little bit? That would be a nice use of some of the skills I had built up over the years, not to mention the thousands of dollars spent on ministry education. What if I led a Bible study, or taught a Sunday school class? I am willing to admit that for a while after I left full-time ministry, our family joined the bagels and brunch club on Sunday morning. I think we were all feeling some trauma from many years of trying to make a broken system work.

Most people realize that the pastor's family participates with the ministry. We see their children in the first row of pews on Sunday and on the youth trips to camp. The pastor's spouse has an almost unofficial role in the church. So, we all needed a bit of a break from the action. But when was the break over? When should we take the kids back to church again? What do I do then in a new season as a former pastor?

I decided to talk to a couple colleagues and put my name on the list of supply preachers. Before very long, I received a phone call from a small church North of Nashville. They were finishing up their pastor search process and needed someone to fill in the pulpit on a particular Sunday as they were waiting for the newly hired pastor to arrive. It sounded to me like the perfect opportunity. The congregation would be excited about new leadership. There was no pressure to perform well. In fact, I told myself, it would be better if I didn't do particularly well so the new preacher could look good when they arrived. I was genuinely excited at the chance to preach God's word again and to bring a little energy and life to worship. It went very well for both of us, myself and the church.

Later, a few other churches reached out and I experienced similar excitement in those experiences. Paula and I began to talk about the possibility of doing more such part-time ministry. It seemed like a good use of my experience and education, as well as an opportunity I was excited about.

To be honest, at the time I didn't personally know many pastors that have done part-time ministry. The only times I had heard of part-time pastors is when a church was dying and that was all they could afford. Truthfully, it hasn't been something that many Presbyterian churches have had to do, as one of the richest denominations in the world. Even new churches often pay a full-time pastor to gather a crowd of Christians before launching something new or building a new church. The idea in those situations is that the full-time pastor will be the instigator of ministry in a particular community and eventually, that ministry would grow into a full-fledged, thriving congregation. This has historically been known as the evangelist model. My mindset about part-time leadership was about to change.

Our real estate business continued to thrive and I was finding my place in the workings of the daily routine. Our family was doing well. There were a few struggles, as Paula and I were now both self-employed, with health insurance coverage and the unpredictability of the real estate market. But it was working, and I did not regret shifting away from church leadership to engage with some new experiences and new challenges. I have always enjoyed learning new things and changing the routine.

In December of 2018, I was contacted by a small congregation, First Presbyterian Church of Spring Hill, TN (FPC). This church was also filling the pulpit following the retirement of a long tenured pastor. He had been their shepherd and their friend for over twenty-five years, and to my knowledge had done an effective job. He and I are still friends and we have spent some time discussing when he too was burned out and frustrated with the role of pastor.

I accepted the chance to come and preach on the second Sunday of Advent. When I arrived at the church early that morning, I was surprised to see just how beautiful the little church was both inside and out. My host for the day, a young member of the Session, escorted me to the church office where we discussed how the service was to go. He was fairly open about the fact they were struggling to figure out what needed to be done, explaining that their former pastor had done almost everything for the congregation.

Most pastors are conscientious and loving people who accepted a call to ministry to serve people and help their churches. It's an obligation that almost every pastor I know takes very seriously. When the congregation is small and the workload is not as heavy as it can be with a larger church, a committed pastor can do almost everything on their own—many do just that.

This was the situation faced by this young Session member. Everything from which key opens what door, to the theological implications of a changing neighborhood, was previously handled by their pastor. Preaching and leading worship went well, and I don't remember if it was before the service or after, but I learned that they needed someone to preach more Sundays and I agreed to fill in. There was something about the little congregation that intrigued me.

Over the course of the next couple of weeks, I learned that the Session of FPC was searching for an interim pastor and wanted to know if I was interested. My answer was yes only if they were considering an option for a part time interim. My last experience in full-time ministry was still too fresh and too painful to even consider going full time again. As a family, we were just starting to recover from the many years of service to the church and the toll that takes on everyone. Still, I was enjoying the idea of serving again enough to further explore it and was even hoping they would consider a limited role.

Much to my surprise, and no doubt the Spirit of God working, the Session was willing to consider the option of a part-time interim pastor. They told me that some in the congregation were skeptical about such an arrangement. Even when the congregation is small, most members of our mainline congregations still hold on to the model in which a full-time pastor is expected. They too are conscientious about the ministry of their congregation and believe that the only way their church can do all of the important things God needs done is with a "fully committed leader."

However, perhaps because the risk with an interim pastor is not as great as with a permanently installed pastor, we were able to come to an agreement: twenty hours a week. This twenty hours would be dispersed across one day in the office, Sunday worship of course, and then the rest of the time spent as necessary to be effective as pastor. My first "official" worship service as interim pastor was to be Christmas Eve of 2018.

I was surprised to find that I was enthused and energized at the possibility of serving as someone's pastor again. Somehow, part-time felt different from the beginning. Because of some early success at FPC, I started to explore more and more the idea that many of our churches would be well served by a pastor who makes their living and cares for their family in a different way from the traditional model, but who still serves as the spiritual leader and resident theologian for a congregation.

There were several questions I knew still needed to be answered. Is it really a different model, or is it just the traditional role with less hours and less pay? Can we engage with the naysayers in our congregation and in every congregation who believe the only real workable model for clergy is to be fully committed and full time? Does this way of being a church affect the other leaders in a congregation and, if so, is that effect positive or negative? Lastly, on a personal level, can I recover from burnout and frustration with ministry and heal my family enough that they too might be open to a different kind of experience of faith?

One thing was certain that Christmas Eve of 2018: I was someone's pastor again. Let's get started.

2

Crisis of Church Leadership Demands Change

"I am about to do a new thing, now it springs forth, do you not perceive it?"

-Isaiah 43;19

The church in North America finds itself in a crisis of leadership. When I was in seminary twenty-five years ago, there was speculation that things were going to have to change. No longer speculation, this crisis is now a lived reality across many denominations and church systems. In my own Presbyterian Church in the United States (PCUSA), our presbytery of 84 churches enrolls almost sixty-five percent of congregations that currently maintain a church roll of less than one hundred members. Eighty percent of those churches have less than two hundred members, meaning that only a handful would be considered medium sized churches by any measure. In addition to this numerical reality, the cost of living is rising in a big way where we live in Middle Tennessee and health care costs are increasing in my denomination's benefit system. All of these factors together add up to less and less of our presbytery churches being able to fill their pulpits with a pastor. In years past, denominational leaders would regularly push for stretching a congregational budget towards a gifted full-time leader that could grow a church, thus paying a full-time salary. But even if growth were more significant than it is currently, it's hard to imagine enough growth over the long term to keep up with the losses of a failing "Christian culture" and our national religious disintegration.

In a telephone survey done by the Pew Research Group in 2018 and 2019, 65% of those interviewed identified themselves as Christian, down by 12% over the previous decade. Additionally, more than 30 million people have changed their religious affiliation to "none" in that same time frame.[2] Church attendance is down as well across all denominations and religious groups. Something important is happening across the religious landscape.

Still there are congregations that seem to be thriving, and in places like Nashville, it would be easy to look around at the mega-churches filled with thousands of people on a Sunday and think that this crisis is just a mainline church problem. That it's confined to old-fashioned churches with outdated or weak theological positions that can no longer attract a crowd. However, what many church experts sense is that mainline churches are simply further along in the process of a massive institutional shift than our non-denominational brothers and sisters. The same changes are coming soon for these congregations as well.

---

[2] "In U.S., Decline of Christianity Continues at Rapid Pace." *Pew Research Center's Religion & Public Life Project*, 9 June 2020, www.pewresearch.org/religion/2019/10/17/in-u-s-decline-of-christianity-continues-at-rapid-pace.

As I'm writing this book, North America and the world is facing a global pandemic and many people are talking of a new reality from what was considered normal before COVID-19. Many churches that were seating thousands of people in large halls and theaters have had to shift their message and their ministry online, leaving empty buildings and unused parking spaces. Usually, enacting massive institution-wide change is like turning an ocean liner, but this time the church has responded to the worldwide pandemic with remarkable flexibility and even resiliency. In just a few months, online worship has become regular practice for most churches rather than just an option for a few, and the churches that were already positioned with technology and expertise have benefited from their advanced work. Good for them.

The question remains, however, what will all of this technology do in changing and shifting the church in general, and more specifically in church leadership? Budgets were already trending towards less giving per member, even for the large mega churches, and it's hard to see how this will not continue or even worsen if worshipers are not able to gather in the building for an extended period. There is no doubt that online worship serves an important role, especially in the midst of the pandemic, but it's also pretty clear that churches will again have to figure out how to do more ministry with less resources.

As good as it has been in helping us weather the storm, what the online worship system cannot do is effectively transition our churches away from a previously dominant clergy-centered model. In fact, online worship may have inadvertently refocused the model back to the clergy. Images of the pastor leading worship with a few music staff members are the only virtual images we saw coming across on our computer screens for months, with limited exceptions. Some churches have done a very effective job of sharing the work of the service, with virtual choirs and praise bands, alternative readers, and sometimes even volunteers offering children's worship. However, most of the worship of smaller churches, which is most of my denominational system, remains very much pastor-centered.

So, we are left again with our clergy, pastors and denominational leaders, trying to figure out what's next. It's not like we haven't been here before. For all of my lifetime, we have turned almost exclusively to our clergy for answers. No matter the size of a congregation or its denominational status, it seems we often consider the opinion of pastors to be the only voices that matter.

I remember attending the Festival of Homiletics when it was hosted in Nashville years ago. It's an annual gathering of preachers and others interested in Biblical interpretation and proclamation. That year we heard the late Phyllis Tickle tell the gathering of pastors and preachers to look around the room. She postulated that the church is going through the very regular five-hundred year "rummage sale"[3] as she called it. Every five-hundred years or so the church makes a massive shift. From the resurrection of Christ to the fall of the Roman Empire in roughly 500 C.E., the church moved from the religion of the empire underground to monastic communities as the dark ages took hold. By 1054, the church had re-emerged and then split with the Great Schism dividing the west under Rome from the eastern church at Constantinople. The next great shift, of course, came in 1519 with Martin Luther and the door of

---

[3] Tickle, Phyllis. *The Great Emergence: How Christianity Is Changing and Why?* Grand Rapids, MI, Baker Books, 2012.

Wittenberg chapel, ushering in the Protestant Reformation with emphasis on learning and reading scripture and sharing the priesthood of all believers. So, if we are on track, then it's time for yet another rummage sale, discarding what is no longer useful to the passage of another five-hundred years. Phyllis invited us to look around at the faces of those gathered in the room. *"You are now making decisions that will affect the next five-hundred years of the church,"* she said.

The challenge inherent in the pastor-centered change theory is that the clergy themselves are so immersed in our system that we aren't able to see outside of it. The opacity of the clergy-industry, in which salaries and benefits care for families and careers, prevents most of our leaders from a willingness to see that we ourselves might be one of the problems. While, as I've said, most pastors are very conscientious men and women who care deeply for their congregations and their calling to serve, those men and women also care just as deeply for their families' well-being. They have children to send to college and mortgage payments to make. It's not very realistic to expect major change to come from those individuals inside of a system they themselves are utterly dependent upon.

That doesn't mean they don't try to make significant changes that improve their churches. In fact, as I confessed in my own journey, clergy burnout is at a crisis moment in North America. Statistics[4] show that seventy-two percent of pastors report working fifty-five to seventy-five hours a week. Eighty-four percent of pastors believe they are on call 24/7. The vast majority use personal and family resources regularly to

---

[4] Statistics provided by The Fuller Institute, George Barna, Lifeway, Schaeffer Institute of Leadership Development, and Pastoral Care Inc.

continue to improve their skills and knowledge. Most pastors feel the pressure of their congregation looking to them for answers.

Pastor Burnout and Leaving

Such reliance on our clergy has created massive stress. Seventy-eight percent of pastors report ministry regularly interrupting family time and vacations. Eighty-percent believe ministry has negatively affected their family and their personal life. Eighty-percent of pastors and eighty-four percent of clergy spouses report feeling unqualified and discouraged one or more times in their career. Such negatives in a helping profession are problematic enough, but with the massive emotional strain ministry takes on clergy and their families, it's clear as a group they would struggle to solve a problem as massive as the leadership crisis in the church today.

COVID has made these statistics for pastors even worse, with a recent study done by the Barna organization determining that the mental health of pastors is declining rapidly. In 2016, just 14% of pastors reported poor or failing mental health, but by April of 2020 that number had jumped to 35%.[5] By August, it was fully 50%. That means if your church currently is served by two or more pastors, one of them might not be doing well.

Perhaps most importantly, ninety percent of pastors report that ministry is totally different than what they thought they would be doing when they first answered the call to serve. These pastors are searching for a way forward along with the rest

---

[5] "COVID-19 Conversations: Many Pastors Are Tired, Overwhelmed and Lonely." *Barna Group*, www.barna.com/research/covid-19-pastor-emotions. Accessed 26 May 2022.

of us that find ourselves in transition when it comes to our congregation.

Transitions Do Not Go Well

Transitioning leadership within congregations is yet another way of telling the story of losses in today's churches. For most of the last few generations, Presbyterian churches have relied on a model for transitioning leadership that heavily relies on the interim pastor system. I, myself have done interim training and served as an interim pastor. The premise of the interim system is based on the idea that a church enjoys a long-term period of leadership stability with a given pastor, who then leaves for retirement or to serve another congregation. The interim pastor is then hired and does important work in a period of instability to solve some unidentified issues within the church or to try and handle any unresolved conflicts that may exist from the previous pastor's departure. The ultimate goal of the interim pastor is to prepare the church and its membership to welcome a new pastor. The hope is to differentiate the previous pastor from the new pastor in a healthy and intentional way, so that the new pastor is able to bring the church to a period of stability under his or her leadership.

The problem in our generation is that many churches never return to a period of stability. The cultural shifts and changes in the religious landscape do not allow such stability, no matter how effective the interim or the new pastor are. Sometimes churches hesitate or go through a lengthy search process to try and get back to stability. Their idea is that careful discernment and the correct process can change the outcome. However, in the North American religious culture, instability is going to happen regardless. To make matters worse, not many new pastors can overcome a long interim period when frustration sets in at how long the process is taking to find the next pastor and members stop attending.

It happens far too often in our system, and even denominations that use a different approach to congregational transition report similar difficulties. In the United Methodist church, for example, pastors are transitioned from the previous pastor to a new pastor in just a couple of weeks. Often, the Bishop preaches one Sunday morning during the transition week to allow one pastor to depart and the other to arrive. This first year of a new pastor in the Methodist system is often considered to be a transition year. A careful analysis in the Kentucky UMC showed that half of all membership losses across all the churches of the conference occur during the transition year.[6] There is enormous stress for a new pastor to perform and lead well in this first year, so as not to create a further deficit the church will have to come back from. The expectation from many in a congregation is that a new pastor is a time of growth for a church, but these numbers suggest something very different.

The not-so-uplifting truth is that churches in various denominations and church systems do not transition leadership well. This is not because the pastors themselves are not capable or chosen correctly, but is instead evidence that choosing a gifted leader is not enough to overcome the massive institutional challenges we are seeing across the board. Many of our churches never recover fully from a time of clergy transition, and periods of great instability are left leading to membership and budget

---

[6] Ray, Teddy. "Tenure and Transition in the Kentucky United Methodist Church – Several Studies." *Teddy Ray*, 5 June 2018, teddyray.com/tenure-transition-kentucky-united-methodist-church-several-studies.

declines sometimes towards the end of a congregation's life.

What's Next?

The pandemic has only exacerbated the shifts that were already occurring long before churches had to close their doors and move online for worship. In the congregation I currently serve, we were unable to host in person worship for the first time in the one hundred and seventy-five-year history of the church. The legacy of our congregation and many others is threatened by the failure to return to regular worship, and the lack of resources for the church budget in light of the pandemic is perhaps the greatest threat to our full-time pastor leadership model. The straw that breaks the camel's back may be upon us.

Thus, the premise of this book and this necessary discussion for all our congregations is how to meet the crisis in leadership that is occurring in our churches. Some of this discussion has been in the making for fifty years and some has been solidified in the last 50 weeks, but change is here now and the time for action is immediate. Over the course of the next few chapters, we will look at whether church growth is possible, and if so, with what leadership models will encourage that growth and change? We will also examine Biblical and historical models for church leadership, like the Apostle Paul. What did John Calvin, the father of Presbyterianism, believe about the role of pastor? Could it really be something other than full-time? What about a part-time model? Finally, we will discuss a few models for alternative leadership, not as something to be replicated but as encouragement to experiment with something different.

As the prophet Isaiah proclaimed so long ago, God is always doing something new. Our challenge is whether or not to perceive it. Change is rarely the enemy of God's people and change that is faithful to God's action might even be described as an opportunity. I believe our current leadership situation might just be the spark the church has needed for a generation or two to create new life and transformational hope. Resurrection, by definition, requires that the old way must die before something new can take its place. May this moment of crisis be dedicated to God's mission to continue to transform all of creation, especially the church.

3

Realistic Expectations for Small Church Growth

"Go therefore and make disciples of all nations, baptizing them in the name of the Father and of the Son and of the Holy Spirit, and teaching them to obey everything that I have commanded you. And remember, I am with you always, to the end of the age."
                                                    -Matthew 28:19-20

I'm not sure when it happened, but many of our smaller churches have stopped believing they could—or even should—grow. In my denomination, over the past four years we have gone from 1.5 million to just over 1.3 million.[7] During that same time, the total number of churches in the denomination also dropped from just over 9,400 to around 9,000 churches. This four-year trend imitates what has been happening in mainline Christianity for the last couple of

---

[7] Statistics on the Presbyterian Church USA can be found at the denominational website, "PC(USA) OGA." *Office of General Assembly*, oga.pcusa.org/section/churchwide-ministries/stats. Accessed 26 May 2022.

decades.

Consistent losses like this have an impact on the psychology of our membership. When our pastors, elders, and even congregations are told we are consistently closing an average of 100 churches per year while only adding 20 new congregations, there is a cumulative effect. Some might call it a self-fulfilling prophecy. Many in our smaller congregations especially have simply given up when it comes to any kind of strategy towards growth. They are in survival mode. When a visitor shows up to worship, sometimes there can even be an overcompensating effect, as members of the church either overwhelm them with greetings or completely ignore them because they just don't know what to do. I believe it's because many of our small churches don't have the confidence in their own ideas about growth and panic when a new face appears in worship.

In fact, many even begin to recite a long list of reasons why the church can no longer grow. These reasons can include: "Our town isn't growing with new people;" or "We don't know anybody that isn't already a part of another congregation;" or "Young people don't like our style of worship;" or even "The programming we offer doesn't interest families with children, who let's face it would be better off going to one of those churches with lots of activities for kids." None of that is true, by the way, but in the absence of both a congregational belief in growth and a leader that believes the church can grow again, it just doesn't happen.

If Not Nashville, Then Where?

As I write this, Nashville as a metropolitan area has been dramatically expanding for most of the last decade. Depending on the statistics you use, somewhere between 75 and 100 people a day move into our area.[8] People in every age demographic and every racial demographic are making the transition to our city. There are young people coming, but so are their parents, following the chance to spend time with their grandchildren. Some of those are unchurched, but many of them have left a congregation back home and will be looking for a new church that is familiar in style and theology. Not all those new residents are looking for a large, highly programmed megachurch. Some would rather be part of a small group of faithful believers that can help them feel at home in a new place.

The truth is there is not a one-size-fits-all vision for any church, and perhaps we miss the gifts God has given to us to be shared with others when we don't confidently reach out with what we have to offer to God's mission in Christ. Every church and every leader in the church should believe they can grow, and more than that, are called by God to reach out with ministry that includes others. Do we still believe in the mission of what God is doing in a particular neighborhood or community? That always includes others. A friend of mine likes to say, "Our problem is that none of our churches have a marketing and sales department any longer." If you no longer believe your congregation has something to offer others, then why are you there?

The hard truth for us in the Nashville area is, if our churches can't grow here, in the midst of a thriving, growing city, then where would we expect the people of God to be able to grow?

Every day we have chances to tell others about the blessings we enjoy from God and the opportunities we share to worship

---

[8] Staff, The Tennessean. "Home." *The Tennessean*, 26 May 2022, eu.tennessean.com.

together and do ministry as a church. We all just need to rediscover the confidence to believe in what God is doing in our congregations, and to be willing to adjust and shift our focus and our leadership to discover some realistic growth.

Do We Believe We Can Grow Anymore?

What is realistic growth for a small congregation? When I first arrived at my last call, a medium-sized urban congregation in Nashville, my associate pastor used to say we were going to grow by 1,000 members in my first year. It was more encouragement than an actual goal. That would have more than doubled the size of our congregation, twice-over, in a single year. While I don't limit the power of God to accomplish amazing things, that was not a very realistic goal. What if instead we had added just 40 new members, or roughly 10% of the congregation? That would have well outpaced any losses we experienced that year and would have given us a positive growth number by year end. That's healthy growth.

In fact, that's healthy growth for another reason too. The congregation would have easily been able to effectively welcome that number of new faces and new families into our congregation.

People that join a congregation want to get involved. They want to find places to plug in and be known. When a church experiences very large growth, it becomes harder for every new person to find their place. Then there exists a revolving door of those that didn't feel welcome and aren't connected to the congregation, resulting in their gifts not being incorporated into the body. That becomes almost impossible when the growth of a church outpaces their capacity to welcome and embrace new members.

In Matthew's gospel, Jesus charged the church to "go and make disciples of every nation."[9] But that's not where it ended. He also commanded the early church to "teach them to obey everything that I have commanded you."[10] Numbers for numbers sake are not enough. We are told by our Lord to make disciples. That requires that we not only welcome new faces, but we help them become part of the church.

Let's consider that 10% number for a much smaller church. What if the church only has 50 members, or even 25? Can you imagine how good it would feel to a small congregation to welcome 5 new people, or even 3? That's a boost to the confidence of those disciples of Jesus to know that God's witness is 5 more than the year before. Then the next year, we might imagine welcoming 6 or 7. I am no mathematician, but that means in just 3 years a small church of 50 members is now at 68 members. In five years, they are at 83. You get the idea.

It should be said that numbers aren't everything when it comes to a church, and growth is not the only measure of a faithful congregation. However, I do think we should confidently believe again and pray that God can grow our congregations, and then do the things that are necessary to welcome new people and new gifts. There is nothing that can change a church culture and long pattern of stagnation faster than a few new faces with some different ideas about how God's blessings might show up. Who better to welcome other newcomers than those that were the last in the door? Each of those new members joined the congregation for a reason, and sharing that reason might connect with someone else too.

---

[9] Matthew 28:19 (NRSV)

[10] Matthew 28:19 (NRSV)

The Growing Need For Small Community

I believe there are many people in our world today that are looking for that small, extended family kind of church. In the rushed, technology driven world of today, it's easy to feel isolated and lonely. In a study done in 2019 by Cigna America,[11] almost 50% of adult Americans reported suffering chronic loneliness. Further, 1 in 4 say they have not one other adult they can really connect with. This is not an age issue either, lest you believe it's just the elderly. The group with the highest reported loneliness scores is Generation Z, those born between 1998 and 2015. A small church affords the lonely a place to feel like they belong, and when connected to its ministry, it can even become a place to thrive. That kind of welcome takes time and effort, but that is what we are called to be and to do in service to God.

I was recently part of a group discussion with pastors wondering about the future of the church post-pandemic. There was a lot of discussion about virtual worship and utilizing all the new technology we have discovered in the last couple of years. We challenged our larger council of presbytery to make resources available for our congregations to upgrade their technology with cameras, computers and software. Then a campus pastor working with college students asked to speak. She cautioned us to be careful about going completely online and told us a story about her students asking, really begging, to meet in person for college ministry. In their world, everything they do is moving online. Classes, meetings with professors and

---

[11] Hilliard, Jena. "Meth Overdoses And Seizures On The Rise." *Addiction Center*, 21 Aug. 2019, www.addictioncenter.com/news/2019/08/gen-z-loneliest-generation.

even other clubs and activities are all suddenly virtual. "Can we please meet in person as an alternative," they asked. It's not just college students. Suddenly our culture hungers and thirsts for in-person contact—and small churches in particular are in a unique position to provide such a blessing. If they do, then numeric and even spiritual growth is possible.

Leading for Growth

This book is about church leadership and the changing nature of how clergy will need to adapt to lead the church into the future. I have found that, sadly, many ordained church leaders are the last disciples in a congregation to believe that growth is possible. It's a combination of too much ownership of the criticism when churches have no growth strategy, and that same lack of personal confidence in growth that every other member of the congregation seems to be afflicted with.

Churches cannot grow if the leader doesn't believe it's possible, and churches also can't grow if the congregation doesn't think it's possible. Both have to believe in growth in order to realize even modest gains. In my experience, search committees sometimes call a pastor to grow the church, especially young families with children, without fully assessing what the congregation might need to do to meet those young families where they are. Children are loud in worship. They sometimes are hard on old furniture and stain the carpet with grape juice. If that's more than the church wants to deal with, then be honest with each other, and don't ask the pastor to try and welcome people that the congregation really has no intention of serving and enjoying. It would be better to reach out to those in the same demographic if that's who a congregation can serve and serve well.

The last thing anyone joining a church wants to be is "the next generation" that will carry the church on after the current members are done with it. Most of the believers I know want to be the church the very day they walk through the door and join. If our congregation is made up of mostly retirees, then see if you can minister to the needs of every retiree with enthusiasm and love of Jesus. Ask the leader to treat others in the same exact way you want to be handled, with respect and authenticity.

On the other hand, if you have a church full of grandparents that would love nothing more than to love on young families that live far away from their own families, then ask your leader to help you with love and service to children as you would if they were your own grandchildren. Most people, even children, can tell if someone really has their best interests in mind and whether they are being adopted for another agenda.

Most church leaders I know want to be effective at growing God's Kingdom and rejoice when they discover a full heart from one of their flock. If a congregation will embrace the confidence to grow and follow a leader that also wants to grow, there is nothing that can stop even a small church from realizing the purposes God has in mind for them. Realistic growth is still not only possible, but really should be the expectation we share as part of God's command to make disciples of every nation no matter how many hours the pastor serves the congregation.

In the next chapter, we are going to talk about a theological model for the church coming from scripture. What was Jesus' vision for growing the church? We will begin to get glimpses of a possible leadership model for such growth. It might look very different from the models we have currently.

Growth is an integral part of the Christian story, from the beginning, and even small churches must find the confidence in God and in themselves to believe they can grow again. It's a simple question: if we can't grow now, then when might we expect to be able to grow?

4

Laboring For The Gospel

He said to them, "The harvest is plentiful, but the laborers are few; therefore ask the Lord of the harvest to send out laborers into his harvest.

-Luke 10:2 (NRSV)

John Juneman wrote, *"Christianity is not only a spiritual reality, but it is a spiritual and physical existence together."*[12] As the world moves more and more towards all things virtual, there is a danger that the Christian life too will fall even more towards only a private spiritual experience with no grounding in the everyday coming and going of people's lives. Especially when the world of ancient scripture is so clearly different from the world in which most of us live.

One of the greatest gifts of my ministry is the doctoral work I have done with Alan Roxburgh and Mark Lau Branson. From these two professors and pastors came my introduction to the

---

[12] "LifeMessage 365." *JOHN JUNEMAN*, www.johnjuneman.com/lifemessage-365.html. Accessed 26 May 2022.

world of the "missional church." The definition of the "missional church" has been distilled and watered down to mean everything, which means it no longer contains the power of its original founding in the work of Bishop Leslie Newbigin. The short description of what I believe missional meant by this great missionary is captured by my denomination's Foundations of Presbyterian Polity. God's Mission is described as, "The good news of the Gospel is that the triune God—Father, Son, and Holy Spirit—creates, redeems, sustains, rules, and transforms all things and all people."[13] I am grateful that this definition and understanding of joining in God's mission was drafted and approved as I too was developing my own sense of ministry in service to such a mission.

In fact, this definition is critical to understanding how we are called to function as Christians, and especially as pastors, if we understand that we serve under the overall umbrella of the mission of God. What we do is not of our own making, or even under our own power, but is part of what God has been doing all along since the beginning verses of Genesis when God created a world in which human beings and God would dwell together. We dwell together with God and we work alongside what God, through the power of the Holy Spirit, is doing right now in the world.

This is the world and the mission Jesus Christ of Nazareth was called into. We don't often think of Jesus as pastor; however, Jesus did lead a group of people to live lives in service to God's mission. The ancient prophecy of Isaiah, captured by Matthew

---

[13] Assembly, The Office The General. *BOOK OF ORDER – THE CONSTITUTION OF THE PRESBYTERIAN CHURCH (U.S.A.) PART II*. THE OFFICE OF THE GENERAL ASSEMBLY, 2022.

in chapter 12 verse 18 and placing on the lips of Jesus, reads, "Here is my servant, whom I have chosen, my beloved, with whom my soul is well pleased. I will put my Spirit upon him, and he will proclaim justice to the Gentiles." Jesus understood his mission in part was to lead followers to a life of service to others, and that life of service was under the authority of God's mission and energized by the Holy Spirit. This is the Lord we follow.

Luke 10 For Leaders

What does that look like in practical terms in today's hustle and technological world? As I studied with Dr. Roxburgh and Dr. Branson, I was re-introduced to Luke 10:1-12 as a fulcrum text around which rotates the richness of gospel ministry for the church. If we can understand what Jesus was calling the seventy to do so long ago, we have an open window to understanding so much of our own calling to ministry. I would refer all of us to a book by Alan J. Roxburgh, "Missional, Joining God in the Neighborhood."[14]

As chapter 10 of Luke opens, we see Jesus appointing seventy of his followers, sending them ahead to all the places Jesus himself would visit. He tells them to go, saying, "The harvest is plentiful, but the laborers are few" (Luke 10:2). Many of us have read these words and immediately spiritualized them to mean that the harvest is a metaphor for the saving of souls. Go out and bring others back to church. Spread the good news, converting men and women, boys and girls to our faith and thereby grow the barns and silos of our churches by reaping such a spiritual

---

[14] Roxburgh, Alan. *Joining God, Remaking Church, Changing the World: The New Shape of the Church in Our Time.* Illustrated, Morehouse Publishing, 2015.

harvest. I admit that for many years this is precisely the way I read and often preached such words.

However, I was introduced to a different understanding under the banner of the missional church. What if Jesus was not commanding a spiritualized sending at all? What if the story is literal? How might that change our view of the way we live our faith?

The reality of the ancient world was very much dominated by an agricultural model of life and family. This too, creates a chasm for many of us in understanding the subtleties of our ancient stories of faith. Many landowners planted their fields, hiring just enough labor to maintain the crop, but without nearly enough to harvest it when that time came. So, there were times when a landowner would need to hire others to come alongside the family, often living with them for weeks during the harvest season. This created an opportunity for Jesus and his followers.

If these seventy entered the labor market for those few weeks of harvest, it would give them an opportunity to dwell with the landowner's household long enough to share something of their lives. This, according to Jesus, would give them the time and the witness they needed to follow through with the rest of what we see in chapter 10. "Whatever house you enter, first say, *'Peace to this house!'* Heal the sick that are there. Say to them, *'the kingdom of God has come near to you.'*"[15]

This was not a "knock on the door" type of evangelism, as we might imagine today, but instead a time of pretty extensive dwelling together with others that created bonds of trust and sharing. It was dependent on the hospitality of the landowners,

---

[15] Luke 10:9 NRSV

not on the hospitality of the followers of Jesus. It required a sense of being vulnerable to strangers and a willingness to be uncomfortable for the purpose of serving other people in Christ's name. This is our best image of what Jesus might have imagined the early work of the church might be.

How Do We Read "Peace to this House?"

This is still the work of Jesus' church. We are still sent out in the very practical, everyday reality of the world in which we live. Christians go to work and to school. We drive our children to lacrosse practice and gymnastics meets. We shop in the grocery store and carry our trash to the curbs. What if every one of these everyday moments were viewed as Jesus sending us out to others?

Who will we encounter as we go? Are there friends in each of those places, co-workers and even strangers that are very different from us? Can we imagine putting ourselves in a position of engaging with them? What if such an engagement is dependent on their hospitality to us and not meeting inside a church building or program?

The truth is, such ministry requires a different mindset compared to what most of us learned in church culture. We are most comfortable with attending church and even volunteering to offer others the fellowship of our faith. Receiving hospitality is less familiar. Moreover, if our calling to share our faith is dependent on receiving hospitality as it seemed to be in Luke 10, then many in our current ranks will not know how to act in such a calling.

If we believe the future of our faith will require some changes and that those changes are more in line with Luke 10 and a missional understanding of faith and life, then our church leadership must begin to grapple with these changes. This is not a set of skills or techniques. It is instead a new pattern of habits and behaviors that need to be agreed upon and then taught to others. This is a way of life that should infect and color every part of our lives, for Jesus name. This is clearly the purview of our current and future pastors. This is what Christian leadership will have to look like to embrace the future.

What makes this move so challenging is that such a shift is a fundamental culture change. It is more than just tweaking around the edges with small, technical improvements. A technical improvement could be a different publisher of curriculum for Bible study, or another type of music in worship. Instead, the changes that are necessary will significantly modify the way we have done church together for generations. As stated earlier, this is the "rummage sale" type of change promised and prophesied by Phyllis Tickle.

The Case for Part-Time Leadership

This book is about celebrating the gifts of alternative models for ministry, and it's time to go ahead and declare what I hope for with such a celebration. I believe part-time ministry might be the leadership model the church needs. Part-time ministry is certainly not new to the church. It has often been used by churches either on the incline from church plant to sustaining a full-time leader, or on the decline as a church struggles to survive and is forced to cut costs. What exists at the core of what we have understood part-time ministry to be about is that it's not the intention of most churches. It's either temporary on the way to something better, or a hard compromise against what many in the congregation wished were different. Part-time ministry has not previously been the ideal model for the church.

However, keeping Luke 10 in mind and the call of Jesus to send us out as disciples to places other than church buildings and programs, what if part-time clergy was the best model for leadership? I am not saying that calling our own congregations into regular worship, Bible study, and even opportunities for fellowship and faith development are not important. They are and will continue to be fundamental ways we share and develop faith. What I am saying is that such ways of being the church are no longer sufficient as a way of being God's people in the world in which we live if we expect to survive and even grow.

Much has changed and most us us are aware of the shifting religious culture with which we live. We can no longer rely on American culture or any other political or national culture to reinforce and develop Christian faith as we did in the past. The days when "everyone" we knew and all our institutions assumed Christian language and practice were the only way to be religious are long gone. That's not sentimentality, and in fact might be an opportunity for the church. It's an bridge to increasing diversity and cultural growth-a necessary answer to the fact that many of our churches have not embraced people that are different. Technology has enabled us to connect with more people in new and different ways. Communities look different today, and perhaps they are more reflective of the Almighty God that created all people. It's up to us to share Jesus Christ as hope and peace with all our neighbors and friends, even those that don't look just like us.

It seems to me that the model of part-time pastoral leadership is a perfect opportunity for our clergy to participate more fully in a Luke 10 and missional church mindset in alternative ways. If the part-time pastor, along with the congregation, gets more used to living in a world that is both physical and spiritual, both inside the church and outside in the community, then perhaps our pastoral leaders will begin to acquire the skills to teach others. How can we depend on our called pastoral leaders to lead us to someplace different when they themselves are just as ill-equipped for the future of ministry being demanded of us all as followers of Jesus?

A part-time pastor by definition is a man or woman that is living in both worlds. They are leading a church, preaching and teaching and offering pastoral care, while at the same time serving another vocation as a disciple of Jesus. This dynamic puts them in a position of vulnerability and learning that can lead to transformation. It is not a compromise towards something better, or a temporary leader until we can get the "real pastor," but instead the perfect fit for what's needed next in our churches. The part-time pastor is one of those seventy sent into the harvest, where the laborers are few to declare peace, to heal and to proclaim that the kingdom of God has drawn near. Part-time pastors and small congregations are uniquely positioned to learn and adapt to what's next in the Christian story.

Pairs Follow Jesus

One last image I believe is relevant for this discussion: notice in Luke 10 that the seventy are sent out "in pairs." I take this to mean that nobody went alone. Instead, Jesus knew that such work was hard and even dangerous. "See I am sending you out like lambs into the midst of wolves."[16] I like to imagine a sort

---

[16] Luke 10:3 NRSV

of avatar[17] for ministry in which one of the pair in this image from Luke is the part-time pastor and the other is a member of his or her congregation. This is not an image in which the clergy have it all figured out and simply call the parishioners to follow after him or her, to do what I do. There are Biblical images in which "follow me" is uttered, but let's remember that Jesus utters those words to clergy and non-clergy together. Both sides follow Jesus. The member of a congregation does not simply follow the pastor, especially in today's changing dynamic in which the pastor likely does not know what to do either.

This ministry is done jointly, with clergy and every member of the church working together side-by-side. There are no longer any full-time experts we can depend on to know where we are going and how we are going to get there. Instead, the gift part-time ministry can afford us, and in line with our Presbyterian Polity, is the shared journey into the future—hand-in-hand, working side by side together. Again, this is not a "less than" model of ministry. Instead, it just might be what the Holy Spirit is calling us to embrace.

In my current church as pastor, I started by telling the congregation that we were co-learners. I had never been a part-time pastor and they had never had a part-time pastor. Neither of us knew what was going to happen or even how best to go about it. Together we would try and figure it out, along with the Spirit of God as our guide.

For many years now, Luke 10 has given me hope for the future of the church. My understanding of the text and its message

---

[17] According to Merriam Webster, an Avatar is "someone who represents a type of person, an idea, or a quality"

to us in our time continues to move and transform me. In the last few years, Luke 10 has become the foundation for a shift from full-time ministry to a part-time model, and I am hoping to convince more of my colleagues as to the value of this model. As we go, we continue to carry the mandates for ministry and the service to God's mission from Luke 10 with us. Jesus said, *"Go on your way."*[18]

---

[18] Luke 10:3 NRSV

II

Part Two

What Does the Pastor Do?

5

Myth of the Full-Time Pastor: Hit and Hope

"To the weak I became weak, so that I might win the weak. I have become all things to all people, that I might by all means save some."

–1 Corinthians 9:22

A few years ago, I attended a meeting of church leaders and overheard a conversation between a pastor and church elder. The elder was asking about some of the other pastors she knew in our city. Each time a name was brought up, the elder would offer sort of a rating on their preaching. Things like, "She is a great preacher," or "He is a nice guy, but not a very good preacher." The pastor was listening and nodding his head in agreement. Then she said something I have not forgotten.

"You know, don't you? *(As if it was patently obvious to all)* Good preaching is the key to a growing and healthy church," she started. "If the preacher is good then the church will grow." She continued by expressing that the opposite is also true, "If the pastor isn't a good preacher, then no matter what else happens, the church is going to fail." She was very confident in her belief, sharing it openly for all around that might be listening, and the pastor continued to nod his head in agreement. He obviously believed he was a good preacher (or maybe had already stopped listening and was just trying to get away).

Hire "Him" (*and it's usually him*) and You Will Grow

There are lots of other such things we tell ourselves as churches when facing the prospect of growing into a healthy church. "The church must have screens at the front to project the words of the music, and not those tired old hymn books." "We have to change the name of our church from the traditional denominational moniker to something more trendy like 'The Fountain.'"

Allowing our members to dress casually when attending church is now an old style change that was very popular a couple decades ago, disavowing formal dress as expected for all church goers.

The challenge of observing such ideas is that very often, we can see the application of these ideas as visible signs of success in congregations that are growing. However, I believe that assigning such ideas as the secret to success are myths when it comes to actual church health and growth. Those churches that are growing and successful might have made some of these changes, but I suggest there is much more going on than just screens and names and what people are wearing.

The preaching ability of the pastor or otherwise as the savior for church growth and health is another one of those myths. For a long time now, as mainline protestant denominations, we have placed too high a value on the role of the preacher. As if the only thing a church has to get "right" is who is on the sign out front as the lead pastor.

Before I go any further, I want to affirm and say that the pastor's role is critical to a successful church. I still believe, as a practicing pastor myself, we have a crucial role to play as the preacher, the teacher and the one offering pastoral care. This is also not to say no pastor should ever be full-time. In fact, there are lots and lots of clergy that effectively serve congregations in such a way. Great job men and women of God! All of this sounds like a confusing contradiction, so let me take this chapter to explain the "myth of the full-time pastor" as the only thing that matters to a healthy and growing congregation.

What my elder friend above was expressing was the desire for the pastor to be the hook for the congregation. He or she is the face or the voice. They bring the so-called "secret sauce" and people just flock in.

More years ago than I like to admit, my wife and I took a group of youth to a large conference in another city. The event was very exciting with loud music, lots of stage lights, and of course a big-name speaker. During the remarks of the speaker, he invited the youth to look around the room at all the adult leaders in the room. You will know the youth pastors, he said, because they are the ones with goatees and tattoos. He was poking fun at the reality that most, if not all of the youth ministers in the room, had adopted a certain identity. I immediately wanted to find a razor and a bathroom sink to take off my chin whiskers. What was clear from his comment was how so many churches had adopted the so-called pied piper model of youth ministry. Just hire a "cool" young youth pastor and the kids will flock in, as if he or she was leading them in with a flute shaped into a tattoo. This is a myth about how to run a successful youth ministry program.

Do we fall into the same trap when it comes to the pastor of the church? For the longest time, search committees have labored for months and even years trying their earnest best to find the "perfect" candidate for their next pastor. The length of pastoral searches today might indicate that we are still following the pastor myth model.

I remember a video from a church I know introducing their new pastor to the congregation. As dramatic music played in the background, the camera started showing only the new pastor's feet and panned upwards as the music came to a crescendo. I started to laugh as I watched, but then quickly began to feel sad for this bright young pastor. How could he ever meet the expectation of this video creator? He was being set up from the beginning as the savior, rather than the person who *works for* the savior.

The reality is that no pastor, no matter how effective they are, will have all the secrets and all the skills to lead a congregation by themselves. Many try very hard because, as has already been said earlier, they are conscientious men and women trying to do the job they have been hired to do. As our culture and our values as a nation continue to shift away from organized religion, it is the pastors called to do ministry alone that are suffering the most. I am aware of far too many of my colleagues and friends in ministry that are literally breaking themselves and their families in service to a congregation and the myth of the "hero pastor."

The truth is, many pastors don't know what to do to grow and maintain the health of the church, even if the congregation expects them to. It was once true in America that if a church had a decent sanctuary with good parking and a preacher that didn't bore everybody to death, it would grow. Sometimes, even if the pastor did bore everyone to death, the church still grew because there were lots of people looking for a church. Every Sunday there were visitors in the pews and it wasn't hard to get them to commit to being members. Times have changed and the church certainly bears the responsibility for its own dysfunction, but today there just aren't that many people looking for a church home, even in growing areas of the country. That's one of the reasons all those aforementioned ideas for church growth are a myth, including all the emphasis we place on the attractive pastor.

Years ago, we collectively became aware of founder and CEO of Apple, Steve Jobs. He was arguably one of the most influential and effective leaders in business history. In fact, when he stepped away from his role at Apple, the company struggled. So, they brought him back again for another tenure of success. This might indicate to some that Jobs was so key to Apple's success that without him the company would fail. But do we really think Jobs was the only person that needed to be engaged and effective at Apple? Like my friend from earlier that proclaimed the only thing the church had to get right was the pastor, one that could preach, and everything else would fall into place. Apple's success wasn't Steve Jobs alone but the illusion that without a once in a generation leader the company would fail. Could everyone in Cupertino, CA just sit back and let Steve Jobs do all the work, from building the computers to selling them and managing the complexity of software and design? Clearly that's not what happened, as I type this on my MacBook Air with music playing from my iPhone through my Air Pods. Even after Jobs died, the success of the company he started continues to thrive.

The church is not much different. The pastor has a key role

to play, just as any leader in such a position does, but they are not the only key to success in the church. It's a myth that the only thing that's important to the church is the effectiveness of the pastor. The truth is that our over-reliance on our clergy is damaging to our churches and also to the faithful men and women laboring to serve.

I have a lot of appreciation for my colleagues in ministry that are fighting the good fight. They are tired and frustrated and not receiving a lot of support from their congregations and their denominations. They are burnt out, again from the poor matching of the skills they bring with the skills that are needed to be successful in the traditional model. The average time a pastor serves in North America is well under 5 years, from 3 to 6 depending on which survey you read. I believe there is a crisis in pastoral leadership due to unrealistic expectations of churches combined with lack of flexibility in the leadership models we use for our clergy. Many faithful pastors are paying the price.

What About My Education and Experience?

One question that comes up almost automatically when proposing that formerly full-time pastors move to part-time is what to do with the seminary education and experience that they've earned over many years. It's a great question and one that deserves some attention.

My wife often teases me with the description: "highly educated, highly underpaid." At least, that's what she used to say prior to my entry into real estate. Things have changed a bit since I became The Reverend Chris Adams, Realtor.

Pastors can sometimes be the most educated members of a community. In my denomination, it's a requirement that an ordained pastor has at minimum a master's degree, and it's not unusual that experienced clergy have a doctoral degree. Why would someone with so much specified education leave the profession they have been prepared for?

The thing is, they aren't leaving the profession by going part-time. Quite the contrary. A blessing of part-time ministry is that a pastor can make a living in a way other than ministry, while at the same time deploying their education in ministry. Sometimes that living can even be greater, or at least as much, as when they were full-time as a pastor. Our hard-earned education is not wasted at all.

How many small congregations would benefit from higher education and experience in their pastor? Many times, small congregations can't pay the salary demanded by someone with a high level of degrees and experience. However, the part-time model affords everyone in the relationship a different financial expectation to work from. Small churches have less pressure to pay a full-time pastor and the pastor can still meet their financial obligations to their family.

That's not to say pastors should only view what we do through the lens of finances or only adopt such a model in hopes of getting rich. But most of our clergy didn't enter the ministry for financial gain and don't maintain that as the goal. It would be nice, dare I say, for pastors to have some financial autonomy just the same.

Education and experience is a blessing no matter who retains it. A sixty-year-old pastor, who has worked faithfully for twenty or thirty years, still might consider moving to part-time to finish out their career. Maybe they can teach school. How wonderful would it be for high school students to have a history teacher with the same credentials as a college professor? Maybe they can start a business. The experience leading a church can often translate well into entrepreneurship. Nothing is wasted from a life of education and experience, even if it's not being used in the church.

Lastly, would we ever say to someone else in the congregation that has been highly educated, "You are too important to waste your education in ministry?" It seems arrogant to argue the opposite. Besides, isn't every disciple of Jesus called to share the blessings of their gifts with the church and the world? Clergy, highly educated or not, should be no exception.

Then There Is Identity

One other significant barrier to adopting the part-time model for both the pastor and the congregation is the sense of identity that is often associated with being a pastor. Many of us that heard a call to ministry have so connected that with our sense of self that, in many ways, being a member of the clergy has become the whole of our identity. To imagine a shift to part-time might feel to some pastors like they are losing their sense of self.

I would like to encourage my fellow clergy that nothing could be further from the truth. In fact, I believe serving a church part-time can be one of the healthiest things a burned-out and tired pastor might do. How many pastors simply walk away from ministry because they see no other way than resignation from their calling? In fact, in 2017 when I left my last full-time call, that's exactly how I felt.

Let's be clear about what it means to be a pastor from an identity sense. As this book has attempted to describe, the role of a pastor is preaching, teaching and offering pastoral care to a congregation. That should be the connection to our identity. Those are the ways we answer our calling and stay faithful to our ordination vows.

In fact, in my tradition, there is nothing about those ordination vows or descriptions of worship leadership that says a thing about full-time or part-time or how the pastor earns a living and cares for their family. Two references that demonstrate the point.

The first are the constitutional questions that affirm the ordination vows taken by pastors. Most of the questions asked and answered when a pastor is ordained are the exact same whether or not a person is being ordained as a lay person or a professional. That in and of itself is instructive to the point about our identity. We are the same as all other ordained leaders in the church. One question is specific to a Minister of the Word and Sacrament:

"*(For minister of the Word and Sacrament) Will you be a faithful minister of the Word and Sacrament, proclaiming the good news in Word and Sacrament, teaching faith and caring for the people? Will you be active in government and discipline, serving councils in the church; and in your ministry will you try and show the love and justice of Jesus Christ?*"[19]

Did you notice that preach, teach, and pastoral care again? Then there is the description of a Minister of the Word and Sacrament (also called a teaching elder) as a defined ordered ministry of the church:

"*Teaching elders (also called ministers of the Word and Sacrament) shall in all things be committed to teaching the faith and*

---

[19] Assembly, The Office The General. BOOK OF ORDER - THE CONSTITUTION OF THE PRESBYTERIAN CHURCH (U.S.A.) PART II. THE OFFICE OF THE GENERAL ASSEMBLY, 2022. W-4.04

equipping the saints for the work of ministry"[20]. *They may serve in a variety of ministries, as authorized by the presbytery. When they serve as preachers and teachers of the Word, they shall preach and teach the faith of the church, so that the people are shaped by the pattern of the gospel and strengthened for witness and service. When they serve at font and table, they shall interpret the mysteries of grace and lift the people's vision toward the hope of God's new creation. When they serve as pastors, they shall support the people in the disciplines of the faith amid the struggles of daily life. When they serve as presbyters, they shall participate in the responsibilities of governance, seeking always to discern the mind of Christ and to build up Christ's body through devotion, debate, and decision."*[21]

There is nothing in the book or order that connects the identity of a pastor with how many hours that pastor serves during the week or how much the pastor is remunerated.

However, in our Christian culture today, lots of other things have crept in to become part of the identity of the pastor. Things like taking care of the finances of a church, caring for the aging building, and administering the staff and the systems. All these have become part of pastoral identity over the years. I have even heard people say that poverty is part of the identity of a pastor. In a discussion about salaries, one Session member commented that the church was paying the pastor too much money. "Aren't pastors supposed to be poor?" was his comment. Again, I would remind us of the vocation of all disciples of Jesus and not just the pastor. There are functional differences to be sure, but poverty

---

[20] Ephesians. 4:12 (NRSV)

[21] Assembly, The Office The General. *BOOK OF ORDER - THE CONSTITUTION OF THE PRESBYTERIAN CHURCH (U.S.A.) PART II.* THE OFFICE OF THE GENERAL ASSEMBLY, 2022. G-2.0501

is no more part of the pastoral identity than it is for every other follower of our Lord.

My identity as a pastor is connected to my ordination vows and the preaching, teaching and pastoral care I offer to my congregation. That's it. My identity as a pastor remains intact even when I am selling real estate, or serving on a volunteer board, on vacation with my family, and in everything else I do. It's the very same for every member of a congregation.

I know pastors that say they couldn't imagine not being a pastor, and I would say yes, I agree. What they mean when they say that is they can't imagine anything other than full-time. My challenge to my clergy colleagues is to recover the true essence of our identity as pastors, and make your identity about the essential gifts of our work, and not hours worked or employment status or even how much money you are called to steward for God's kingdom.

Recently, I was presenting some of my ideas about going the part-time route to another congregation in my presbytery. This group of leaders were trying hard to wrap their heads around how the pastor could do something outside the church while at the same time serving Jesus Christ in ministry. One member of that council boldly reminded those ordained elders that they too were under the same ordination vows and mandates to serve. "Aren't you still an elder when you are at work?" Our identity as a child of God and a disciple of Jesus remains intact when we are at work, and when we are at school, and even when we are at a Friday night football game.

The truth is all members of a congregation have an identity in Christ and a vocation as a disciple. No matter how they make their living, each is also called to share their gifts. Our Christian identity remains intact no matter where we are or what we are doing. The pastor is no different.

Visitors Respond Most to the Spirit of a Congregation

I love it when our members share their gifts. An example from my congregation is Ruby and her chocolate cake. Ruby is an older member of our church that loves to bake. Years ago, she decided to volunteer to bake for the blood drive that is held at our church. She bakes an incredible cake, I know personally. Ruby has been doing this for years, and the number of people that have been inside our church, in large part because of that cake, is amazing. Don't get me wrong, they are coming to give blood. However, the hospitality of Ruby and her cake keeps them coming back month after month. There is nothing I could say or do as the pastor that could even compete with Ruby's cake, no matter how gifted I am. If I were to get in the way of that cake, I might be giving blood whether I intended to or not.

This is just one small example of how one member of our congregation maintains her identity as a follower of Jesus, no matter what she is doing. She isn't paid to back that cake. It's not her full-time job to provide sweets to the blood drive. Yet, she is an effective witness that benefits our church because she has made baking a part of her expression of faith.

Hit and Hope

I grew up playing golf, but I have never been very good at it. Golf in particular takes a lot of practice and skill to be successful. For me, I never invested the time or the lessons, so when I play golf it's more of a "hit and hope" type deal. I don't really know how to aim. When I select a club, I'm not really calibrated to know how far the ball will travel if I am able to make good contact. Most of the time, because I play so rarely, I am not very familiar with the course I am playing and the layout of the hole in play. So, I just stand at the ball, hit it as best I can and hope for the best. As you can imagine, my scorecard is not much to brag about.

The myth of a leadership model in which we depend only on the gifted, full-time pastor to do everything for a congregation is kind of like this. It's been years since the success of the pastor directly translated to the success of a growing and healthy congregation. We don't engage our members very well in the vital functioning of our churches. We fail to take the time to address our context for ministry and what skills and resources we must serve the mission of God. Members do not understand their identity as connected to the vocation of ministry, no matter where they are at work, at school or even at play. So, because we don't know what else to do, we simply hire a full-time pastor and hope for the best. The record of our successful and growing churches isn't much to brag about either.

I would like to take a minute and invite us to say a prayer for our overworked, over-functioning pastors and their families. One of my goals and my hopes for this book is that some of them will see part-time ministry as a balm of Gilead, enabling them to continue to use the gifts they have given to God and their identity as a pastor in a way that is more sustainable and healthier. I would also hope presbyteries, boards, and bishops might also see the part-time model as a more viable and healthy alternative to thinking church growth and health is solely about finding the right pastor. It's a huge blessing when the burden of knowing what to do next in ministry is a shared burden with other members of a congregation. Pastors, you will still have a critical role to play in your church, but it will be a more balanced and healthier role. After all, you are still just human beings created in the image of God and given the identity as a follower of Jesus Christ first, pastor second.

Next, we will discuss Pastor Paul and what his example might have to teach us about faithful leadership in the church as pastors. By any measure, Paul was not a full-time, salaried pastor with a large office and lots of authority. He was a follower of Jesus with a big heart and a passion for spreading the good news of the gospel far and wide in the ancient world. We would not be a church today, as Jew and Gentile, if Paul had not had an imagination for leadership and a growth strategy for the church. We can learn a great deal about what we might do as leaders when we imitate how Paul and others planted and served congregations.

6

Part-Time Pastor Paul

Paul went to see them, and, because he was of the same trade, he stayed with them, and they worked together—by trade they were tent makers. Every sabbath he would argue in the synagogue and would try to convince Jews and Greeks.

–Acts 18:2-4

Most Christians today would identify Paul as an evangelist and a pastor. We know of his missionary journeys across modern day Greece and Turkey. Our hearts break with the early, first century Christian community, as we imagine the suffering of the Apostle Paul. He was imprisoned, beaten, shipwrecked, and traveled perhaps as many miles as any ancient person ever did.

Most pastors and church members admire his courage and his drive to spread the gospel of Jesus Christ far and wide. In fact, if it weren't for Paul, most of us that currently call ourselves Christian would not be in a position to do so. Christianity would likely have died out as a minor sect of Judaism. However, through the power of the Holy Spirit, Paul took the Christian faith to the Gentiles, and we are all beneficiaries of his faithful work.

But what kind of pastor was Paul? I wonder how many of our pastoral leaders today think of themselves when they think of Paul as pastor. It's common to misunderstand who Paul was when coming from a Western European mindset. Did Paul preach and teach? Did he administer the sacraments? Did he make sure the building was unlocked on Sunday morning, before the early risers could beat him to church for Sunday school? Was Paul a good church administrator? Or was Paul's idea of the role of pastor different from ours? It's clear that our idea of pastor was not the same idea Paul had about his role in the church.

Plant With A Strong Work Ethic

Paul never refers to himself as pastor. He only uses the word once in all his writings, and even then, he is only using the word to refer to the way a shepherd tends to a flock of sheep. In 1 Corinthians 9, Paul talks about the rights of an apostle and uses the image of one (pastor) *"Who tends a flock and does not get any of its milk?"*[22] It's a coincidence of language that brings the words shepherd and pastor together for Paul, rather than being indicative of the way he saw his role in the early church.

Paul, however, uses plenty of familial language throughout his letters. He often refers to other believers as brothers and sisters. He seems to understand the early church as a close-knit group of believers that are mutually obligated to one another through their allegiance and devotion to Christ, similar to a biological family. For example, in Paul's first letter to the Thessalonians he refers to the believers in Thessalonica as

---

[22] 1 Corinthians 9:7 (NRSV)

"brothers and sisters" over and over again, naming them as special to he and the other evangelists and giving thanks for them almost like a parent would do with their own children. In chapter 2, verse 11, Paul writes, *"As you know, we dealt with each one of you like a father with his children, urging and encouraging you and pleading that you lead a life worthy of God, who calls you into his own kingdom and glory."*[23] Not only does Paul see the community as siblings together, he seems to identify with the idea of being their father in faith. He sees himself as responsible for how they will "grow up" in their following of Jesus the Christ.

Catholic priests later being referred to as "Father" has roots in Paul's understanding of the pastoral task. The early monastic communities perhaps picked up this language to describe the cloistered way they were living out the faith, as brothers and sisters. The Abbott and Abbotess in monastic communities would come to be known as the father or mother of the group, meaning they were responsible for the training and care of the monks or nuns of the monastery. The term monk comes from the Greek word "single or solitary," but when monks lived together in community, the Pauline, familial language seems to have been adopted including the Abbott as father. The same is true in a convent. As the faith developed and the idea of a pastor as the caretaker of a community of faith took root, the title of Father seems to have come along with the role for all those serving congregations, or village churches in Europe. Today, there are still Christian traditions, such as Roman Catholic, Orthodox, and Anglican Protestant congregations that have maintained the title of Father for their clergy.

---

[23] 1 Thessalonians 1:11 (NRSV)

Empower Leaders

That's not to say the idea of Paul as pastor in the way we understand that term is accurate—it's really not. Paul did not see himself as a professional caretaker of congregations, as most today with the title of father would. Rather, to Paul, he was an evangelist with gifts to encourage the planting of a community of Christ. He was called to raise that community in the faith until such a time as they could live it on their own, without him.

In fact, some scholars like Scott McKinney have pointed out that Paul's leadership model was directly connected to the Jewish family model of teaching, encouraging, correcting, and nurturing. This is arguably the way Paul saw his leadership role in the early church.

In his book, *Pastor Paul*,[24] Mckinney introduces the concept, credited to Paul, of "Christoformity." This was the idea that Paul saw his job as father to teach others to imitate Christ in the same way that he and the other evangelists did. Everything for Paul started with living out his faith and he saw his role as leader was to create an environment for Christ-like spiritual formation. Paul was the mediator. His job was to put those in the community in a new mindset through teaching—one that would go far beyond his own understanding and practice of faith, led only by Christ himself. He encouraged them with his rhetoric and his letters after he left them. Paul even corrected his community when he saw them going astray. In Corinthians, we see his warnings around observing the shared meal.[25] Finally, Paul offered grace first. The same grace that

---

[24] Rosner, Brian, et al. *Paul as Pastor.* Reprint, T&T Clark, 2019.

[25] 1 Corinthians 11:27-34 25 Acts 9:1-31 (NRSV)

he discovered on the road to Damascus was his constant re-gift to the church. Simply, Paul's concept of fatherhood was to raise his children with Christoformity through his teaching, encouraging, correcting and nurturing.

Let's use a comparison of images that might help illuminate what kind of father Paul would have been. Think of Paul as more of a family farm father than a trust fund father. These are surely gross generalizations and not meant to be descriptive or to assign a value to either, but rather to illustrate a point.

Consider a rural farm father, whose intention is to raise his children on that very farm so that he can leave them the farm and have it continue without him. The assumption is that the father will teach his children and encourage them to work alongside him, learning how to farm for themselves, and then one day the children will take it over completely and do the same work without the father.

Compare that to a productive business-man father who has been successful in making and investing money. So much so, he is able to leave his children enough resources to take care of themselves without having to work in the same way the father has had to work or at all. In essence, the trust fund father has done the work, so the children don't have to. You see the difference?

Paul was much more like the first father than the second. He visited an area, sharing the gospel in a way that made sense to the residents and their culture. If they were Jewish, he taught them as a Jew. If they were Gentiles, then he adjusted his pitch to make sense to them. He lived alongside the newly converted "children" for as long as was necessary to teach them and encourage them to live the faith on their own. Then, when Paul was satisfied that they could lead a community of believers without him, he moved on to another place, leaving leaders behind to continue in his stead.

Today, in many of our churches, it seems we have leaders that serve more in the way of a business-man father. We assume that the work of the church should fall solely on this "father" in ways that mean the average member doesn't have to do everything in the practice of faith. It's almost like we think that if the pastor is successful enough at faith, then he or she might cover for the rest of us—that we can live off the faithful work of a few professionals and experience the blessings of a healthy faith in God. I don't believe that's true; yet many of my colleagues continue to serve in models of clergy leadership that more closely resemble the trust-fund father than the family farm father.

What if the pastor of a congregation saw themselves more in the way Paul saw himself as a church leader? Our job is not to do the ministry for our community, asking for an occasional check for support or a raise in our remuneration. Instead, what if we saw ourselves as the father or mother that raises our children not to need us? So that when we are gone, or even while we still remain, the faith can increase beyond our abilities and expectations. Many of us have understood for a long time that the success of our ministry is measured much more by what happens after we leave then while we are still there.

Paul was a hard-working, lead-by-example kind of pastor. He used his talents and gifts as a craftsman and seamster. Each day he went to the market to sew and to represent his wares. Therefore, he was not dependent on the community for his salary, but more importantly he was out in the community in the same space and time where his "children" were living out their faith.

Paul knew what it was like to work hard. He understood economics and the business of the marketplace. He was no doubt skilled at selling and talking with people. So, Paul could maintain a sort of equality with his flock that many pastors today can't. By equality I mean that Paul wasn't on a pulpit, or pedestal as some regard the position to be, but rather out among his people. He was like that farm father that worked in the field with his children, leading them by example and demonstrating each and every day the way farming was to be done. Paul did the same when it came to Christian living.

Do you want to see how a Christian conducts his business, spends his money, and talks to his friends and colleagues? Just watch Paul to see it demonstrated. Paul didn't just talk the talk. He also walked the walk.

Move On

Pastor Paul's focus seems to have been on building up the community of believers in such a way that he could then continue his journey and spread the gospel. The economic models of the ancient world, in which Paul and other craftsmen were able to stay in an area just long enough to do all the available business of that region before having to move ahead to another area for more business, made it possible, and even necessary, for Paul to travel.

The advantage this created, whether Paul knew this at the time or not, was that he was able to avoid most of the obligatory relationships that we see created today in many churches. This eliminated the so-called "we can only be successful with this pastor or that pastor" mentality so prevalent in today's church culture. Paul's communities knew he was with them for a limited time and then he would move on. That model of church leadership was healthy in that it was built up around shared leadership. "When Paul leaves, here are the ones he has trained and endorsed for us." This operates the same as, "when dad dies, it's our job to carry on the family farm."

It's amazing to see how far Paul traveled and how many communities of faith counted him as the father of their Christoformity. It would be an amazing Bible study, now that we have explored the way Paul led his communities as pastor, to read each of his letters, keeping in mind that family farm father idea. What would we see differently in Paul's calling and encouragement of faith that we miss when we don't read his leadership in such a way?

Work Hard, Empower Your Leaders, Move On!

Let's turn finally in this chapter to the practical application of what we can learn from Paul about being a part-time pastor. I suggest there are three main points.

The first is imitating Paul's work ethic in our own practice of church leadership. Hard work is healthy, just as rest and enjoyment is healthy. Many parishioners in our congregations work hard, some extremely so, and our ability to identify with them in working harder ourselves to make ministry work better is something that can improve our connection with those we are called to lead. Having to make a living in another way, other than from the church, is not a distraction or less than the work we do in the church. For Paul, there was real value in hard work.It's what enabled him to travel to a place and to reside there long enough to work with other Christians. If Luke 10 is a model for the church, then living alongside working people so that they can learn your practices and habits is what Paul would have demonstrated for us.

Sometimes the job of clergy has been identified as a profession, and clearly there is education and professional training that makes it so. However, we should never lose sight of the value of everyday hard work to bring us side-by-side with men and women that we can minister to while working. Our job is people-centered first and foremost, and most people I know work hard. When we consider our work ethic as a bi-vocational or part-time pastor, we might be able to look to Paul as our mentor.

Second, if we are to limit our over-functioning as clergy, we should focus on creating Christian believers that can live their faith with or without us. Paul's laser focus seems to be on imitating Christ and teaching others to do the same. Our job is not to do the work of the church for our members and even other staff members, but to do our part encouraging others to do theirs. Like a baseball team manager who makes sure every position is filled and successful, our job is not to play all the positions but to encourage the team that shares the journey with us. Being a part-time pastor creates this as a necessity—and we as pastors and our churches are healthier because of it.

I once knew a pastor colleague that seemed to revel in teaching other pastors how to be a better preacher and teacher than he was. He would often talk about how much fun it was to see them catch up to him and then pass him by, leaving him in the dust. There was no ego in this old pastor's heart, but he truly celebrated when others lived the faith he loved so much. Perhaps this too is a model for us to consider when leading our congregations. Paul wrote, *"make my joy complete: be of the same mind, having the same love, being in full accord and of one mind. Do nothing from selfish ambition or conceit, but in humility regard others as better than yourselves. Let each of you look not to your own interests, but to the interests of others. Let the same mind be in you that was in Christ Jesus."*[26] When our congregation embodies this message, then we have truly led them to a sense of Christoformity.

Finally, if we can imagine ourselves even as working ourselves out of a job as a pastor, or passing along a family inheritance, then maybe we can do the things every day that truly empower and encourage others. The truth is, there are some things the community counts on us and our training and education to bring. Preaching, teaching, and pastoral care are the unique gifts we bring. But much of what else a pastor does are not unique gifts or a unique calling. Others can do those things far better than we can and we should imagine they will do those things whether we are there or not.

One of the great joys of my current call is arriving on Sunday morning to discover all the things that the congregation has done to maintain the church and its activities that week while I was not there. The paraments were changed. The flower beds were cleaned out and mulched. The new Sunday school curriculum was ordered and delivered. The food dropped off for the food bank was delivered. I could go on and on. It's fun for me as the pastor to know that all those things happened without even my knowledge, let alone my request or my planning. It's one of the marks I count when I consider just how successful this congregation would be even if I wasn't there. It requires some letting go of control, which is hard for some of us as pastors to do, but the payoff is so worth it. Nothing will make you smile more than seeing your congregation empowered by Christ more than by your own power to lead them.

---

[26] Philippians 2:3-5 (NRSV)

Work hard. Empower your leaders. Move on. That's Paul's model for leadership as a pastor and it's one that endorses part-time and bi-vocational ministry pastors.

Of course Paul is not the only model we might look to for guidance on how to effectively pastor a congregation. Next, let's jump ahead about fifteen-hundred years to another pastor that would be seen by most as effective and skilled. John Calvin was a pastor in Geneva, Switzerland and a reformer of our faith. What can Calvin show us about the role of pastor?

7

Pastor John Calvin was Focused Local Theologian

Stay awake and pray that you may not come into the time of trial; the spirit indeed is willing, but the flesh is weak."

-Matthew 26:41

"**T**heology is about waking up."[27] So writes Clemens Sedmak in his book, *Doing Local Theology; A Guide for Artisans of a New Humanity*. In an age when so many are invested in mindfulness and the practice of being more attuned to the world around us, the idea of theology as waking up might make sense to many in our culture. In fact, as the subtitle of his book indicates, a new humanity would benefit again from those among us that can help us think theologically. That is to think about God. Not in the academic sense, as so many think when considering theology. We imagine cold dark libraries where scholars pour over the writings of the church fathers. Instead, what if theology was done with a sense of wonder and

---

[27] *Doing Local Theology: A Guide for Artisans of a New Humanity (Faith and Cultures)* by Sedmak, Clemens(February 4, 2003) Paperback. Orbis Books, 2003.

imagination, almost as if it were the work of children. Sedmak writes further, *"Doing theology in the spirit of children means seeking God in all things, being aware of God's presence, listening to God's voice, and being attentive to the signs of the times. We can do that only if we wake up."*[28]

It sounds funny to say, given all we know about the seemingly intellectual and even austere Calvin, but I believe this way of theology and wonder is one way we might see John Calvin and his role as a pastor. As part-time pastors, perhaps challenging our congregations to theology and wonder becomes another primary method of our work.

To say Calvin was controversial would be an understatement to say the least. To those that loved him, he was a hero of epic proportions. His students and imitators claimed that he was irreplaceable as a systematic theologian and a Christian mentor. To those that hated him, and there were lots of those that wrote harshly of Calvin, he was an inflexible authoritarian, whose only other quality was his superior ego. The purpose of this discussion is not to decide whether John Calvin was a nice person or not, but instead to try and explore how Calvin saw his role as a pastor for the churches he served. John Calvin served churches in France and in Geneva, being called back to the same church in Geneva for a second time.

Preach

Herman Selderhuis writes that Calvin thought the life of a Christian was a battle—an extremely difficult pilgrimage as the

---

[28] *Doing Local Theology: A Guide for Artisans of a New Humanity (Faith and Cultures) by Sedmak, Clemens(February 4, 2003) Paperback.* Orbis Books, 2003.

believer wearily struggled to get to his final home in heaven.[29] Calvin would have enjoyed J.R.R. Tolkien's books about the little Hobbit that answers the knock on his door with an epic and dangerous journey for the ring. Calvin lived at a time in history in which life was a struggle for survival against disease, poverty, and war. It's perhaps why he worked so hard in Geneva to create a social safety net for his neighbors and fellow citizens, and didn't just proclaim the gospel with words. To Calvin, the work of the Christian gospel was to help pilgrims along the perilous journey of life.

However, before he was a town administrator and reformer, Calvin was a local theologian first and foremost. He believed that the role of a pastor given to him and to others was focused in the task of helping a congregation see the wonder and mystery of God all around them. Calvin was one who believed faith could be arranged in a consistent pattern of thought.

We know him first as the lawyer that wrote a systematic way to think about theology. This was his vision as a reformer. His pastoral vision, though, seems to have been more about a relationship with God. His goal was to bring his parishioners into a meaningful understanding of who they were in relation to God and who God was in relation to them. We can hear this in his sermons. *"Calvin's 'pastoral vision,' that is, his view of the priority of God and a relationship that all human beings must have with him in either friendship or judgment, permeates the Institutes and makes it intensely relevant for us."*[30]

---

[29] Selderhuis, Herman. *John Calvin: A Pilgrim's Life*. 1st ed., IVP Academic, 2009.

[30] Hearne, Travis. "'The Word Did It All': The Necessity of Preaching According to the Protestant Reformers." *Southern Equip*, 18 Jan. 2022, equip.sbts.edu/article/the-word-did-it-all-the-necessity-of-preaching-according-to-the-protestant-reformers.

Teach

From this history, it's apparent that Calvin believed pastors are local theologians that are called through systematic teaching to train other members in the church to be the same. He was like that "artisan for a new humanity" that Sedmak identifies and demonstrated in his own pastoral work that the work of a theologian and the role of a pastor must not be separated. The pastor's task is essential to the growth, edification, and perseverance of the church.[31] There is much more to say about Calvin, and in fact, many books have been written about John Calvin the pastor. Our need in this moment is not to analyze the entire body of his work or the talent he brought as a theologian any further. What is useful would be to accept the premise that Calvin believed himself to be a local theologian and teacher, surrounded by a congregation of local theologians, to see how this approach of theology and wonder might inspire us as part-time clergy leading congregations.

One of the things I have learned in doing part-time work and being involved in different vocations is the benefit of seeing the world around us through multiple perspectives. When one works only as a pastor, it's easy to begin to fall into the trap of seeing everything only through the lens of a pastor. We can get silo-ed with tunnel vision and lose the ability to see things as others see them. If we are going to do theology in a local community and call others to such work, then we need to have a fairly large lens in which to wonder about God.

When I first started in my last full-time call, my associate pastor had been at the church for a few years already. He was

---

[31] Greef, Wulfert De. *The Writings of John Calvin, Expanded Edition: An Introductory Guide.* Expanded, Westminster John Knox Press, 2008.

aware that I came to that call with fresh eyes and could see things he was no longer able to see from inside the system. We agreed that it would be important to make some decisions about new things while I was still able to identify them as an outsider. He knew I still had a larger view of the congregation than he had, having been at the church for a number of years. Before long, we both knew that I too had become accustomed to the congregation in ways that left me unable to see as I once could. It was a lesson I have not forgotten about: our inability sometimes to see the world around us from inside the pastor's office. It's not a criticism of pastors and the pastoral office, but simply an observation that we can become insulated from other realities when our only reality is that of a clergy person.

The benefit of part-time ministry is that we regularly move from inside the system to outside the system. We go from one career to another. We work in the so-called "secular" world and then transition back to the "sacred." Each time we are able to explore theology from a new perspective. Our lens is wider than just our clerical office. This movement can become the engine for our wonder.

Pastoral Care

"Pastor John Calvin involved himself in the merchant trade and economics in Geneva. Calvin saw the possibility of turning it into a city with the industry of hard work and honest gain."[32] Calvin believed his industry and work offered him the best

---

[32] "John Calvin: Theologian, Pastor, and Social Reformer – by Dr. C. Matthew McMahon | Reformed Theology at A Puritan's Mind." *APM*, www.apuritansmind.com/the-reformation/john-calvin-theologian-pastor-and-social-reformer-by-dr-c-matthew-mcmahon. Accessed 26 May 2022.

opportunity at social reform. He did not draw lines of distinction between the secular and the sacred in Geneva, much like our world does today, but rather thought of industry informing his faith, and vice versa. For Calvin it was all theology and wonder. This way of life was the driving force in how John Calvin did pastoral care as well.

In fact, Calvin in particular believed the theology of pastoral care was to ensure the effectiveness of the Christian witness in a community. Pastoral care was not to be just another member of the helping professions, one given the "spiritual dimension" of such care. For Calvin, praying for healing and health for his members was for their comfort and peace, but also so that they could continue to use the gifts trusted to them uniquely by God. A sick saint was a missing gift in a community, and so Calvin went about taking care of them with energy and love. His pastoral care was primarily theological in nature, and not in a cold, academic sense. Rather, his care for his congregation derived from the way Calvin understood his vocation as a theologian.

Preach, Teach, Pastoral Care

As we consider the opportunities given to us as part-time pastors and theologians, I wonder if this mindset would be helpful. In whatever way we choose to make our living outside the church, there are surely theological implications and instigation we can bring from that part of our lives. A quote often falsely attributed to St. Franci of Assissi captures the totality of our way of life: "Preach the gospel at all times, use words is necessary." In all our vocations, we are called to explore where the gospel and our work intersect. If we are a teacher, then let the innovations of education impact the way we teach about

God. If we work in healthcare, are there best practices for caring for our community as Jesus would that transfer to the ways we take care of our congregation? It's a more holistic approach.

For me as a Realtor, it has been amazing how often my work with clients buying and selling homes transfers to my work as a pastor. That might seem strange at first glance.

For example, the way we communicate in our business has offered us some different ways to communicate with the congregation I serve. In real estate, it's important to almost over-communicate with clients, so they always know what's happening with their current or future home and so they have an open channel to ask questions and know the process. One of the criticisms real estate agents sometimes hear is that clients don't know where they are in the process or they feel isolated without the power of knowing what's next. In the church, this criticism is also sometimes the same. Many church members complain that they aren't aware of what the church is doing or how they can be a part of the process of ministry. My work in real estate has improved my desire and my skills to communicate effectively with the congregation. It's a theological issue to consider every member of a church worthy of connecting to what the larger body is doing. We are more effective when the men and women in our churches feel they are part of what is happening in profound ways.

Another example: we have been taught to run our business with what's known as a "red light/green light" model. When we have resources to spend, it's a green light to invest in the business. When the light is red, however, we don't spend hoping the resources will show up. In the church, our theology indicates that we depend on God to provide for us and some would advocate that we invest our resources believing God will make up the difference. I don't disagree. However, when the church is limited in resources, it's at least an appropriate time to evaluate whether what's being spent is necessary or not.

There are lots of other examples, but perhaps the best one is this: as a Realtor, we run our business almost exclusively by referral. We have been blessed enough not to have to make a ton of cold calls or create mass marketing campaigns. There have been many surveys done over the years that report that most of the people that visit our congregations know someone already in that church. One study reported over 80% of visitors are there, not because of a sign or an internet ad, but because they were invited by someone in the congregation. The theology of this is that God uses people, flesh and blood incarnations of Jesus Christ, to spread the gospel and share the worship experience. Would it not make sense to see lessons of a referral-based real estate business for a referral-based church? It has made a huge difference to us.

We encourage our members to proudly invite their friends to what we are doing, and I believe the enthusiasm of our congregation to do that is a great measure of how we are doing in growing the church. If God can use flesh and blood to spread the word about the value of a successful real estate business, then surely God can use the members of a congregation to grow the Body of Christ.

Calvin inspired his congregations through preaching, teaching and pastoral care to do local theology, to be the church and do the work of the church. This included the command in the gospel of Matthew to make disciples of all nations.[33] Do our members believe this is their theological vocation? Do they see

---

[33] Matthew 28:19 (NRSV)

themselves as the primary movers when it comes to growing the congregation and calling others to join in God's mission and the church's ministry? Or is it only up to the full-time, paid clergy to do?

If Paul was the empowering, Christocentric teacher, then Calvin was the local theologian focused on preaching, teaching and pastoral care. Both men functioned well as pastors and leaders for the church. In the next chapter, we will include these two primary gifts in a broader discussion of all the gifts necessary for a pastor to function well in the part-time model.

8

Helpful and Not: Pastoral Gifts

"The gifts he gave were that some would be apostles, some prophets, some evangelists, some pastors and teachers, to equip the saints for the work of ministry, for building up the body of Christ,"
-Ephesians 4:11-12

Up to this point, much of what has been discussed has been broad and even theoretical. This has provided a basis for the remainder of the book, so that you might understand where the specifics and practical aspects of the work of a part-time pastor are located both practically and theologically. What follows might best be described as the beginnings of a manual of operations for churches and also for pastors wanting to explore further the implications of moving to a part-time model for ministry.

To begin, let's imagine what a church would look like when led by a part-time shepherd? Some questions begin to arise. First, what are the essential gifts needed in a pastor in order to do the ministry of our congregation? If the time a pastor has to serve a congregation is intentionally limited, what do we want the pastor to focus their limited time around? If a pastor is to be effective and feel successful in their vocation, what should they spend time with on a daily basis and what should the congregation see as faithful service?

Second, how would we structure the schedule, both the church and the pastor's, in order to realize the benefits of a new model? What blessings does technology afford us, especially in light of the pandemic, that make it possible to adjust our expectations about the "office hours" a pastor is expected to keep? Does part-time signify simply limited office hours or should we expect that we might not see our part-time pastor every Sunday?

Finally, what attitude might a congregation bring to help ensure the success of this new way of doing things? Is this something we are excited about as a new model for thriving in ministry or do we already have preconceived notions of what part-time ministry looks like, both as clergy and congregations? The approach to this work will greatly determine its success.

Essential Gifts

Our discussion of the work of Paul and John Calvin instructs us on what these two congregational leaders believed to be the essential gifts for ministry. Paul wanted to teach and empower the members of his congregations to become leaders in the faith, so that they could take over once he moved on to plant new churches as well as bring others in the community into a relationship with Christ.

Calvin thought of himself as a local theologian, given the blessing of theological training and a point of view that oriented him and his community to what God was doing in the world around them. Calvin believed pastoral care was uniquely oriented around theological and existential questions to help members of his congregations in need to see God as fundamental to healing and peace.

It should be noted that motivating, teaching and even theology seem at first like things we are doing for or to other people. This orientation can put our pastors in sort of a hierarchical mindset when it comes to those they are really serving alongside. Maybe thinking of Paul and Calvin as models reinforces such an idea further? Traditionally, theologians wouldn't see either of these two in any other way but as hierarchical "church fathers." However, I would challenge us to think of these essential gifts as those we can only perform with others, and thus a humble living out of our spiritual gifts together with others that are doing the same. Jesus himself warned us about seeing our leadership as anything other than collaborative.

"But Jesus called them to him and said, 'You know that the rulers of the Gentiles lord it over them, and their great ones are tyrants over them. It will not be so among you; but whoever wishes to be great among you must be your servant, and whoever wishes to be first among you must be your slave; just as the Son of Man came not to be served but to serve, and to give his life a ransom for many."[34]

So, it would seem that if a pastor is going to thrive in a part-time role, they need a couple of essential gifts as they collaborate with others. There are of course lots of other gifts we bring to our work, but let's consider just three as perhaps essential: motivating a congregation (which might also be called preaching), teaching, and finally doing theology as an expression of pastoral care, not only for members of the congregation, but also for the community. These should sound familiar from previous chapters.

---

[34] Matthew 20:25-28 (NRSV)

First and foremost, the part-time pastor needs the ability to motivate and energize others to take on their Christian vocation. Of course, this is done under the power and authority of the Spirit of God. If it is working with youth and children, then how can the pastor encourage the adults in a congregation to serve faithfully with enthusiasm and love. If it is feeding the hungry in service, or taking good care of the church grounds, the empowered-by-the-Holy-Spirit pastor can empower others to lead. There are lots of other abilities in a congregation. If a member's gift is financial ability, empower said member of the church to lead with collecting and using the church's resources. If the gift is care of others, then how can the pastor empower a member to give Christian love and care for another? And on and on...

If you are a pastor, currently full-time or part-time, that still believes the old adage, "if you want something done right you have to do it yourself," then I may doubt how effective you will transition into a part-time role. Preaching the presence of Jesus Christ into the midst of a congregation is the power that enables a congregation and its members to thrive.

Jesus preached over and over that all were welcome in the Kingdom of God, not just as receivers but also as participants. Every member is important to the ministry of every church, and pastors and preachers motivate others through the energy and the power of the Holy Spirit. We all want to see ministry excellence in the congregations we serve. However, it's an essential gift that part-time pastors see participation by members of their churches as a method for excellence. A volunteer might not perform a task the way we would do it—however, the gift they offer to their church and their Lord is more important than our control over how something gets done.

The truth is, many of our clergy struggle with issues around control. In most cases, it's not our fault. Full control is the way many of us were trained in seminary and early in our careers, when the church was very different. Congregations had more resources, and they were able to hire "professionals" to do the work of ministry on their behalf. We were expected to provide "professional excellence" in the programs delivered and the ministry provided to our congregations. In fact, I would argue there is even a way to preach that maintains control and authority over a congregation, different from the kind of preaching that shares and motivates. There is a much longer discussion about whether or not "professional excellence" was helpful practice to our ever-reforming churches, but it really doesn't matter. We don't have to see that as a failure in order to make a shift to something new.

The reality today is that many of our churches can no longer afford to continue to hire all they need to do their ministry and now must rely on volunteers. As a result, clergy have to be willing to let go of some of our control and the way we would do it in favor of sharing the work with the members we serve alongside. Preaching to energize and motivate others to serve is an essential gift of a part-time pastor.

Second, pastors need the ability to teach and do it effectively. The Christian life is a counter-cultural orientation to life that is a gift of the Spirit. At times it requires the believer to live by a different set of standards or to give grace when others won't. It necessitates a shepherd or a mentor to help a group of new believers to understand. Like the Ethiopian Eunuch from the court of Candace said in response to Peter's question about his understanding when reading the scriptures, "How can I, unless someone guides me?"[35] It's true for both experienced Christians and for those newly converted. Congregations depend on the ability of their pastor to teach. The pastor is not the only teacher, but a significant role of the part-time pastor is to be a theologically trained teacher of the faith.

Finally and related, our pastors must retain their vocation to think theologically about their communities and the lives of their members. In our denominational system, all pastors have to be theologically trained. In part because of our history, Presbyterians place a high value on education, so we train and educate our ordained clergy and our commissioned lay pastors. It's really an amazing blessing to be given the skills and the time to think about God in such ways. It's also a blessing to be with others at critical times in their lives to reflect theologically about what an event might mean. This applies to sickness and tragedy, but also to celebrations of birth and marriage and growing up.

It wasn't that long ago that clergy were included on the boards of businesses and community organizations. The reason such appointments were made was to keep the community aligned with God. To bring theology from the church to the main street, so to speak. To be truthful, sometimes there were other less than faithful reasons to include clergy in such ways but for this discussion let's go with the optimistic, theological one. Ethics and generous practices were part of the mandate of clergy on such boards, but clergy also had a voice in the evolution of small towns and how corporate decisions would impact the well-being of citizens. Thinking theologically is what we expected of our pastors and that theological mindset was given for the pastoral care of a community.

---

[35] Acts 8:31 (NRSV)

As we emerge from hopefully the darkest days of the pandemic, I have reflected on my position as pastor during such strange times. When I preached and taught about what life was like with COVID-19, I could do it not just as a faith leader and pastor of a congregation, but also as a business owner. How do we make payroll when the world has shut down? How do my members make ends meet when their monthly paycheck has stopped? Is it okay to apply for help when it's offered in a crisis, and what's the responsibility to give back? How do we honor the men and women who still have to work when others can shelter at home? These are just some of the questions that came up. Each of these are theological questions as well as pastoral ones, and the clergy are the ones in every community charged with raising them.

Perhaps an essential gift is to ask that our clergy return to such involvement in the neighborhoods in which they serve. Rather than just run the church and its programs for members and friends, we might ask our clergy to be involved in more outside church activities. Being part-time requires that clergy be outside the church as much as they are inside, which places them in yet another gifted position. They can think theologically with leaders and members in the congregation while at the very same time, think theologically in the way they are making their living.

To some that might seem counter-intuitive. How can part-time clergy be more involved in the community than when they were full-time. It's very simple. Because when a pastor is part-time, they are already engaged in the community in important and meaningful ways. Even if the job they do outside the church seems less than critical in a community, the fact that a part-time pastor is interacting with people and systems outside the church places them in a different position than simply inside the role of a full-time member of the clergy. It is also important that other members of a congregation function well, to afford the pastor the time away from the church to do such work.

I learned a long time ago that the definition of burnout for a pastor is not when there is too much work to do and not enough time to do it. True burnout happens when there is a poor match between what gifts a person brings to the organization and the tasks they are expected to perform. We all know people that run circles around us in activity and never seem to get burned out. Could it be that the essential gifts we have traditionally asked of our pastors are not a good match and that's why we are seeing an epidemic of burnout in the clergy? Getting focused on the gifts truly necessary for our part-time clergy is essential for the success of our churches and those relationships.

This chapter is not meant to be an exhaustive list of gifts. Each congregation needs to deal with its own context in discovering what else is necessary for a leader to serve them and do it well. It's critical that the gifts of the pastor match the congregation's compelling mission from God. However, I would suggest that effective teaching, motivational preaching, and theologically grounded pastoral care are important for every pastor, but especially essential for our part-time clergy where focus is needed to thrive.

A "Healthy" Schedule

When I first arrived at First Presbyterian Church, there were mixed feelings about hiring a part-time pastor. I was told the Session had sent out a survey asking about "part-time" as an option, and the votes were split. This was not surprising to me, given the fact that the church had never had a part-time pastor before. For generations, even when the church was struggling with financial and membership numbers, a priority had always been to keep the pastor fully employed. The congregation believed this was the obligation of a faithful membership, which I really appreciate. In a world that seems anemic when it comes to honoring commitments, a small group of Christians who set a priority to work and give to keep the pastor fully employed is admirable.

It was clear to me right from the beginning of my part-time arrangement what was at stake. So, I made a commitment of my own. It was simply this: when the phone rang and I could see it was a church member on the caller ID, I just answered it. If possible, even if I was with family or a real estate client, I would simply try and be available. It's pretty easy actually, in today's world, to answer and just tell someone when you will call them back. That's what most people expect. They don't have to talk to you right now, but they would like to know when they might expect to talk with you.

The same applied when it came to the multitude of other ways people communicated with me. If someone sent a text message, I responded. If it was an email, before the end of the day they got a reply. I believe that if someone sends an email, they don't believe it to be so urgent that it can't wait until the end of the day. However, they do expect to hear from me and most days it's not hard to respond before ending the workday. Facebook messages? Same response time. Are there times when I miss my mark and responses go longer than I want? Sure, but my intention as a matter of practice was to try and be available to the congregation. Humbly, I dare say it worked!

What many of those early skeptics of part-time ministry commented on was that when they called or sent me a message,

I actually responded. When they called me on the phone, I answered the phone. No secretary or voicemail to leave a message, I answered. After all, don't most of us have our phones with us all the time? This is not some specially guarded clergy secret, but something most of us would say is fairly basic.

The amazing thing about communication is the expectations we set. If you are open to being available most of the time, then people will allow you tremendous grace in your response. We live in a world of more and more communication with less and less actual communicating. Even though this is basic, I wonder if such a practice of answering when called is both counter-cultural and a modeling what responsiveness might look like for the community of Christ. Can we imagine Jesus sending your phone call to voicemail? How frustrating would it have been to call Paul and be told "the voicemail has not been set up, please try your call later?" Yet, how many times do we get those responses from others in the world in which we live?

I should say, again with a little embarrassment, that this was "renewed" learning for me. To be as honest and transparent as I can be, I have not always done things like this. In fact, when I was full time in ministry, it might have been days before someone got a phone call from me.

Emails piled up. I convinced myself that a text message to someone, even if it was something really important, was okay. It's not. Most people want to talk to someone when a crisis is occurring, and it's not okay for us just to be too busy. I think a lot of pastors facing burnout and struggling numbers in their congregation are often guilty of the same thing. It's hard to be available when we don't feel affirmed and confident in what we are doing.

Someday I would like to write another book about the power

of voice and personal communication as the incarnational presence of Jesus Christ for all involved, both caller and called, but that's not for now. I'll just leave it to say through real estate and business I learned again how important it is to take phone calls and how to honor the power of personal contact. Another benefit of my part-time schedule and clergy life.

With this as background, we turn to some best practices when it comes to the schedule of a part-time pastor. It's perhaps important to set a couple times during the week when members and friends of the congregation know they can find the pastor in the church office. Some will likely make it a point to come by and visit with you to share a cup of coffee. Others will identify that time on their calendars when they can meet with the pastor for something they need to talk about. It's key to publish office hours and to try and try and stick with them. Things will come up, but try and be where you say you are going to be when you say you are going to be there.

However, I don't think office hours need to be the majority of the time the pastor should be working. Sunday worship requires fixed timing. Office hours should be honored. After that, however, my recommendation would be to allow the pastor to determine how best to serve the congregation and from where. Visiting the hospital, attending a community meeting, and writing a sermon from home or at the local coffee shop are examples of things best done off campus at the pastor's discretion. If we don't trust that the pastor is working during those times, then there are much larger issues at stake than the weekly schedule.

The good news about our life and times with technology is that even when the pastor is not in the office, they are still available. We don't need to belabor the point any further, except to say the days when it was necessary for a pastor to be in the church office to be effective are long over. Setting our expectations about the weekly schedule will be key in the success of the pastor, as will the expectations the pastor brings to how they should effectively communicate.

The last thing to consider when thinking about a healthy schedule for a pastor is the number of Sundays we might expect from a part-time pastor. Perhaps we start with a question: should part-time mean more than just part-time office hours during the week? Do we expect that the part-time pastor will be there as many Sundays as a full-time pastor?

Again, I draw an example from my own life. A real estate agent doesn't just work Monday through Friday. There are routinely Saturday and Sunday showing of property and other tasks related to the buying and selling of a home. That means, as a part-time pastor, I am juggling work schedules every weekend. In addition, I have a family and kids who have their own schedules, fall breaks and spring breaks and other weekend obligations to consider.

If part-time ministry is going to be a sustainable option for someone like me, then it's going to have to have some flexibility in the number of weekends I need to prepare to preach and lead worship. In my current situation, the congregation and I have agreed that I would have at least one Sunday a month off, with someone else leading worship so I can be away. The church budget takes into account paying someone to fill the pulpit in my absence. Even with this additional cost and also hiring another part-time staff person to do other types of ministry, our budget for personnel is still far below what it would be if I were full time.

My family and business partners sit down at the beginning of the year and plan the calendar to the best of our ability to take advantage of such a schedule. The church knows when they can expect for me to be away, and I can make plans to be with family, participate in work conferences and special events, and to rest from the busyness of all the ways I feel called to serve.

There are other ways to do this too. If a part-time pastor is a schoolteacher that has summers off, they might want to do their schedule differently, building in the times they know they will have off. If the other career of a pastor is a tax accountant, then maybe they need more time off during tax season. Maybe a football coach needs time expectations set around the season. There are hundreds, if not thousands, of ways to do this. The important thing is to set the right expectations from the beginning so every member of the church knows what the plan is, and then can adjust. I still believe most people in our world today are flexible if we are willing to trust them with the information they need.

In my Presbytery of Middle Tennessee, we have spent a lot of time over the past few years talking about the need to be more flexible with our pastors and our church leadership. The time has come to walk that walk and to talk that talk, and carefully examining the pastor's schedule is one way of practicing that flexibility.

Recently, I spoke to a group of pastors and other church leaders about my experience in leading a congregation as a part-time pastor. They asked me if I believed this model was sustainable for me and for others that might embrace it. My answer was, in part, about the expectations of the schedule we expect of such pastors. If part-time only means less hours in the office, then it's probably not going to work for many pastors. However, if we can be more flexible in setting our expectations for a healthy schedule, then I honestly believe this model is more sustainable than our current full-time model.

The most profound thing happened to me personally during all this new understanding of communicating and scheduling. When the burden of full-time was lifted, and when I was no longer responsible for everything that happened in the church, then suddenly I found myself more available with less effort. It sounds strange, but focusing on preaching, teaching and pastoral care only suddenly opened my heart to the needs of my congregation in ways I could not have imagined. It was no longer a frustration or a hardship to be available to my congregation, and to answer the phone or email or text, even at times like holidays or vacations. Suddenly and strangely, it became an honor again to be present with them when they reached out. It's a little hard to explain, and might be one of those things a pastor has to experience to understand, but the part-time model with less work hours created more availability than I had ever had in ministry prior. It's a gift you have to open to see.

Attitude

The last gift a pastor can share with their congregation is a healthy attitude when it comes to the work they do, both inside their congregations as well as out in the community. Again, I have learned from my personal experience that attitude is infectious, whether good or bad. If the pastor is burned out, overworked and feeling like their gifts are not being welcomed or used effectively, then very often they will be grouchy and not encouraging of others. However, if the pastor is excited about the way they spend their days, both inside and outside the congregation, then that will also be translated to others.

Consider the late Steve Irwin, known affectionately as "The Crocodile Hunter" by his millions of adoring fans. Have you ever seen a more enthusiastic person? Irwin's passion was sharing his love and knowledge about animals. At first, his fame happened because he was so excited about crocodiles, arguably an animal nobody would find very exciting. Terrifying, yes. Exciting, not so much. But Irwin was always so excited about his work and his sharing with others that he won over the hearts and minds of millions of people. For most of my life, I was scared of snakes, but after watching episode after episode of Irwin calling them "little beauties," my attitude began to change. If he could be so excited, how could I not be?

The reality is positive attitude comes from using the right gifts with the right balance of time and energy. When we as pastors get that right, it's amazing what can happen in our congregations. When church leadership works with the pastor to ensure the right balance, they are improving the chances that the whole leadership model might be successful. Preaching is more creative and energizing, teaching is Christ-focused and engaging, and pastoral care comes with the compassion and love of Christ.

Essential gifts, deployed with a healthy schedule, and a positive attitude can truly transform a church and beyond.

III

Part Three

Blessing the Gift of Part-Time Ministry

9

You Can Do This!

"Awe came upon everyone, because many wonders and signs were being done by the apostles. All who believed were together and had all things in common; they would sell their possessions and goods and distribute the proceeds to all, as any had need. Day by day, as they spent much time together in the temple, they broke bread at home and ate their food with glad and generous hearts, praising God and having the goodwill of all the people. And day by day the Lord added to their number those who were being saved."

–Acts 2:43-47

Use your imagination for a few minutes...
You drive into church on a Sunday morning and notice that the parking lot is mostly full.

After finding your spot, your kids jump out of the car almost before it comes to a stop and rush into the building. It always brings a smile to your face when you realize how blessed you are that your kids love coming to church.

You make your way to the Fellowship Hall to the coffee pot. Every week, Rose is there making coffee, offered with a smile and a warm greeting. Rose is one of the friendliest and warmest people you have ever met and she's giving out more than coffee to those arriving at church. Rose is also an amazing baker and cook, and she brings homemade goodies to go along with the coffee. Each week, you and lots of others can't wait to arrive to see what sweet surprise Rose has brought.

You make your way down the hall, greeting others that are also smiling, to your Sunday school class. As you arrive, Sung greets you by name, just as he does every Sunday. Sung is a retired executive that has literally traveled the world. He loves the Bible and can bring it to life like no other person you have ever met. He's so thrilled to be teaching, even when he references Leviticus and Obadiah. He starts the class by inviting prayer concerns, and then prays aloud as if God is in the room. Sometimes the hair stands up on the back of your neck when Sung is either teaching or praying. There's always something important to remember when class is over.

As you make your way back into the hallway, you notice that your oldest child is talking to her Sunday school teacher, Sandy, as they walk towards the Sanctuary. Sandy teaches school at the local High School and she also coaches soccer. She and her husband don't have any children of their own, and she is one of the best mentors for kids you have ever seen. She knows how to connect with your oldest, even when other adults don't. It's been a rough couple of months for your son and having someone like Sandy in his life has made a huge difference for him and for you. You are not sure what they are talking about, but you know it's something hopeful and energizing because that's just who Sandy is. It's amazing how much better things are when Sandy is around.

It's almost time for worship to start. As you get close to the doors, you can hear one of the ushers, Spencer, calling out your name. "Hey, how did that big presentation go at work on Thursday?" he asks. "I said a little prayer for you on Thursday morning, but I'm sure you didn't need it. I'm sure you wowed them with your ideas!" You appreciate that he remembered—it was a pretty big deal for you and the idea that someone was saying a prayer means a lot. Spencer always has a joke ready for your kids. "Hey y'all did you know there are cars in the Bible? All the disciples were of one Accord." Even though the joke is corny, when Spencer starts to laugh, nobody, including the kids, can help but laugh too.

Your daughter wants to know if she can sit with Mrs. Massey again this week. Mr. Massey passed away from cancer just a few months ago, and she doesn't want her to have to sit by herself. The Masseys had been youth advisors for years and the kids loved them both. When your daughter was going through middle school a few years ago and having a lot of trouble with friends, Mrs. Massey came to lunch at school at least once a week to help her. She's always dressed like a model in a skater magazine, something that other kids notice right away. Your daughter's connection with other girls was dramatically helped by Mrs. Massey's attendance at lunch. What makes you even more proud of her is that your daughter is now returning the favor by helping her feel less alone. Where did she learn how to do that?

When you finally get to your seat and look up towards the front, you can see that Kenny is hurriedly finishing with the baptismal font. Kenny is a free spirit. He loves to kayak and mountain bike and all things outdoors. He brings small stones from one of his favorite streams nearby, carefully cleans and chooses the best ones, and places them in the font. Each time there is a baptism, after the service every member is invited to come to the font and take a stone home with them. It's a reminder that the child or adult that was baptized belongs to all of us as a community of Christ followers. Kenny says it reminds him of how he takes a little pebble from all the parks he visits, and how connected we are to each other and to the earth. You remember you have a jar full of those little stones at home, each one representing a baptism in the church.

It's time for worship to start, and the choir files in from the doors at the front. Evelyn is at her usual place right in front, smiling from ear to ear as she processes. Evelyn was born with Down Syndrome. She can sing like a professional opera singer. Normally she hides her face and won't make eye contact, but when she opens her mouth to sing, it brings tears to the eyes of all that can hear. It's been amazing to watch the choir director, Brian, work at Evelyn's confidence and singing. He is so patient and passionate about music. It's almost like people are treated for whatever ails them with the gift of singing and music. Some of the songs they sing are old, but what happens to people through Brian's music seems like it's new every week.

Joanie starts the service with announcements. She is the Betty White of announcements. No matter what she is talking about, it's offered with so much enthusiasm and even humor that you can't help but be excited about it. Who knew cleaning out the flower beds and mulching them could have the power to take the place of sleeping in on Saturday morning, even for teenagers?

The children's moment is brought by Christina, one of the smallest women you have ever seen. Most of the fourth graders are taller than she is, but that doesn't stop her from reaching them with a message about Jesus and God's love. Everybody's favorite is when she brings one of her animals into the sanctuary for a story about life and times on the farm where she lives with her wife Kim. Chickens, ducks, and even a pot-bellied pig have all been guests up front, to the delight of the children.

Every Sunday, the church brings a story about something the congregation is doing in the community, and today it's brought in by Marco. Marco stands at the front of the church holding what appears to be a bundle of green beans. He explains that the cannery will only use beans of a certain size and the beans he is holding are going to be thrown away. Marco has organized a way to save these beans from the trash, to wash and process them in the church kitchen and to give them to our local food bank. You take out your calendar and schedule your time to help. You can wash beans you think—it reminds you of your grandmother and her garden anyway. That brings a smile.

When it's time for the scripture lesson, Ed rises from his pew and walks to the front. Ed is a giant of a man, who looks a little like Shaquille O'Neil. He immediately commands the attention of everyone in the sanctuary, which is further reinforced by the sound of his voice. He dramatically bellows through the scripture lesson, and it's almost as if God were reading it in worship. Ed's wife Georgia teases him, saying he practices in front of the mirror to be sure he enunciates all the names with perfection. It works. It's amazing!

Then it's time for the pastor to take her place in the pulpit for today's message...

The Healthiest Churches Have Everyone Participating

Pause your imagination for a minute and rejoin me for our conversation about the power of part-time ministry. Notice how many church members, saints of God, have been referenced before we even mention the pastor. I count twelve. That's a good number.

The point of this is to notice how healthy a church can sound when lots and lots of people are participating and not just the professional staff. Isn't this a church many of us would love to be part of? From delicious coffeecake to reading scripture like James Earl Jones, members of every church have gifts and skills to bring to ministry. When the pastor is the only one expected to share gifts on a Sunday morning, the ministry of the congregation is only as broad and wide as the gifts of the pastor. But when lots of people share, the gifts multiply like the loaves and the fishes. That's exciting to be a part of. Notice I didn't reference the decor of the sanctuary or the style of worship. There was no mention of the sign outside the building or even how many people were in attendance. What is important is that those that were there were connected to each other and connected to the sharing of their gifts with God and the community.

There are times when things are exciting and fun. There are also times when things in a church are sad, like the loss of a beloved youth leader. There are those to whom the sharing of gifts are easy and those that have to work at it. But no matter how easy or hard, what's important is that every member of the church be hopeful, engaged, and selflessly serving.

You can do this! I fully believe the way to get more people engaged in ministry is for our clergy to stop over functioning under the heavy burden of heroic ministry. If we allow them, the conscientious pastor will try and fill in the holes of ministry themselves, and this well-meaning practice deprives someone else from sharing their gift and thus realizing the fullness of their relationship with God.

Maybe it's easier for the pastor to have donuts and coffee catered professionally and delivered to the church, but then

Rose wouldn't have a ministry. Surely the pastor is the most qualified to teach Sunday school, but then we would miss out on the amazing gifts shared by Sung. Nobody can read scripture like Ed, not even the pastor, and would we not miss out on the "voice of God" if the pastor took this over too?

Churches, my advocacy for part-time pastors serving churches is not just about the pastor. In fact, it's mostly not about the pastor. I have tried to lay out a case in which the pastor is more healthy and more engaged with members and in the community when part-time. I have argued for the essential gifts of a pastor as a more focused way to do ministry, focusing on communication and engagement with people and not programs. Lastly, I want to turn to the blessing this model can offer to every member of every congregation.

Said simply, if the pastor doesn't do everything in a congregation, then lots of others get the chance to join with God through Jesus Christ with meaningful and important service. This is true with other professional staff.

Ministry Systems Make Sure Everyone Works

Years ago, my wife and I volunteered to do youth ministry. I've lost the name of the book from which this idea came, but I remember the point. We were taught to ask one simple question when it came to doing ministry with youth. The question was, "Is this something the youth can do for themselves or not?" That evaluation was based on safety and capacity. A 14-year-old youth cannot drive themselves to a mission project in another city to repair houses or serve meals. It was also based on realizing the gifts of the youth themselves. If we did everything for them, then they can't do things for themselves and their own spiritual lives, and the ministry suffers.

The same principle applies to adults. If the pastor does a task that someone else in the congregation can do, sometimes better than the pastor, then the church is hobbled from the use of one of its best gifts.

If you are willing to take a risk and to limit the overfunctioning of your pastor, the payoff in terms of the sharing of gifts is potentially huge. My example above contains only the things my limited experience could imagine as part of a typical Sunday. There are likely millions and millions of other stories we could tell, and that's the promise of the church for the future.

You can do this. More accurately stated, God can do this. I believe God wants healthy and fulfilled pastors—those that work earning a living in something they love while also sharing their love with God's church. I believe God wants the world to realize the fullness of the expression of gifts in every congregation, no matter how large or small. I believe God intends to make every church thrive with enthusiasm and energy, so that hearts, families and even the world is transformed. Together, with God's help, we can do this.

10

What's It Look Like? Some Models for Ministry Leadership

"That same day Jesus went out of the house and sat by the lake. Such large crowds gathered around him that he got into a boat and sat in it, while all the people stood on the shore."

–Matthew 13:1,2

One of the earliest models for the ministry of Jesus happened by the seashore. Jesus was preaching and teaching and healing, and so large crowds followed him. One day, as he sat by the Sea of Galilee, a large crowd gathered around him and so he had to teach his parables while sitting in a boat just off the shore. To this day, there are churches all over the world with ceilings that mimic the ribs of a small wooden boat. The idea of the church as a boat full of Jesus has become a model for what the church of Jesus Christ might look like. There are many, many others.

For our purposes, I want to suggest some models to consider when a congregation is interested in implementing a part-time model as an alternative to the traditional model of full-time pastoral ministry. Perhaps it goes without saying that these are just a couple of suggestions, and in no way a comprehensive list. My hope is that thinking about a couple of examples might instigate a congregation onward to use their own creativity and risk in finding what works best for them.

Let's consider just three ideas for part-time ministry. The first is the half-time or 20 hours per week pastor. Second, let's consider what I know to be called the HUB model for ministry, one in which several people share the leadership of a pastor. Finally, when it comes to church planting or starting a congregation, what if the model was something other than finding some land, building and church and hiring a pastor? Creativity is the key in all models for ministry leadership and any of these models can be modified and built upon.

20 hours *per week*

Perhaps the most traditional and well-known model for part-time leadership in the church is the so-called, half-time pastor. This is the model referenced earlier that is often deployed either as a church is just getting started or when it's time to offer a congregation palliative care as it dies. There are lots and lots of examples of pastors who have faithfully led through this model, and when I started this conversation several years ago, I was reminded of just how many have trod this path before me. In fact, this is the model often named "tent makers" after the ministry of the Apostle Paul who it's assumed worked half his time in ministry and half his time as a craftsman.

The first thing to say when considering this model is to encourage all our churches considering such a plan to reach out and find those pastors and leaders that have already done it successfully. You won't have to look very far, and I would guess that if you are willing to buy the coffee, you might just get all you can digest in best practices and even things to avoid.

This model is also my current context. I can share just some of the highlights of what I have learned, but I am still a newbie in the world of tent-maker ministry, so this is not meant to be prescriptive.

In this model for ministry, the church recognizes a difference in what's required of their pastor. This model is intended for those that will make their living, at least in part, from another source, leaving the duties and responsibilities of the pastorate to work in conjunction with their other job.

Other than a restriction in time and commensurate adjustments in the job description, this is still a fairly typical pastoral role. As described prior, the duties of the 20-hour-per-week pastor are still primarily to preach, to teach, and to do pastoral care. In some traditions, this will also include the responsibility of the denomination's polity to lead the sacraments and to moderate whatever council leads the church.

What most members and friends of the congregation will see is that this person is the pastor of the congregation, albeit with less hours and more shared responsibility with others. This pastor will continue to be identified in the community as the pastor. Other staff members can be hired as the church grows but this model suggests that there is one pastor of the congregation and others that fill other roles.

In the next chapter, I will discuss some best practices when it comes to all the models of part-time ministry such as hiring, compensation, schedules, evaluation, and sustainability. For now, this is but one way of organizing a pastor's duties around the concept of part-time.

HUB Model of Ministry

Recently in our Presbytery of Middle Tennessee, in partnership with church consultants Ministry Architects,[36] we experimented with a leadership model that was new for most of us.

The pastor at Woodland Presbyterian Church in East Nashville retired after nearly thirty years of ministry. The congregation had held its own during those years, and was a champion of gay rights, the homeless, and folks in need in our city. It was an important witness, too important to fail. Many of us knew without some innovation it was likely the congregation would falter in the leadership transition.

So, we decided to be creative in our approach. East Nashville is an especially fast-growing area of Nashville, due in large part to the increase of millennial and other young adults. To reach this demographic, in an aging building in need of repair and renovation, our core belief was that young people should be led by young people.

We decided not to hire a full-time interim pastor, with tasks beyond any one person's ability and skill set. Instead, we created a shared leadership team model in which anywhere from six to ten young adults all share the duties of pastor. We called it the Hub after the idea of a device that helps to connect multiple computers on a shared network. This is a very part-time model and those serving have been seminary students, recent graduates of universities in our city, and those with interest in the profession of ministry. There have also been those that were just excited about what we were trying to do and wanted to help.

Each member of the team, affectionately called "Hubbers,"

---

[36] https://ministryarchitects.com/

is given an area of responsibility. Some preach and some teach. We need administrative help, musicians and youth and children experience. Each week the group meets around the table on Sunday morning to coordinate the work of the church, to ensure no person or ministry slips through the cracks. It takes an intentional approach to coordinate and to schedule, but in the end it has worked. The church is growing again, especially with the millennial demographic. This is particularly important given the pandemic and the fact that the city of Nashville was shut down for worship for well over a year.

There is a new energy created when churches consider some experimentation in leadership. With any experiment, there are times when things don't go as planned and those opportunities are for learning and reshaping our efforts. The Hubbers have come and gone, and in this model of part-time leadership, a church should expect that there will be lots of coming and going. Hubber positions are not meant to be career positions and once someone gets some experience, our hope is that they can move on to other places sharing what they have learned and experienced. It's like a giant learning lab for flexible leadership models and actual church experience.

Woodland has become an exciting place to do ministry together, and it might be a model you and your church can rift off of in order to create something that works for your congregation.

In our presbytery, we have since adopted a similar model for two other churches, including a bilingual Latinx congregation in another part of our city. Four Spanish speaking pastors lead this congregation and have even started a feeding program out of this shared leadership model. We are still learning from the HUB model, but from this willingness to step outside of the norms of the way Presbyterians often do, we are grateful to God for the successes we have already enjoyed.

Church Planting

Many denominational executives and church leaders have noted the desperate need to plant more new churches. With the number of congregations closing their doors on an annual basis, combined with continuing demographic growth in the USA, some experts predict the need for between 400,000 and 500,000 new churches by 2050.

This comes at a time when so many existing congregations are struggling to survive. I have laid out in a previous chapter my own presbytery's numbers. Eighty percent of our churches are less than 200 members, and the number of members in most of those congregations is falling year by year. In the old days in my denomination, church planting was done by presbyteries and larger churches with resources. It took a lot of resources to start a new congregation.

The model was to carefully choose a growing area that was perhaps under-served by a church. The presbytery purchased land in such an area and started construction on a worship space. Sometimes this was a flexible space that could serve as sanctuary as well as fellowship hall. Finally, the presbytery or another church would hire a full-time pastor and set that founding pastor to work in the neighborhood growing a Sunday morning crowd.

Over the years, as religious demographics have changed dramatically in North America, it's no longer a very feasible or cost-effective strategy. In fact, denominations and other church groups that still plant churches this way have a very high failure rate and have built that into the increasing cost of planting new churches. Almost like religious venture capitalists, they invest resources of time and money, knowing that many of their ventures will not become congregations that last beyond the initial founding phase and that's just the price of "doing business" in the post-modern religious arena. However, for many of us this seems like a waste of limited resources, and a better way seems like something to search for.

What if church-planting teams and others interested in new congregations started out by hiring a young couple currently living in a neighborhood where a church plant might be likely? The pay could be very part-time at first, or even to help cover the rising costs of healthcare or childcare. The idea would be for these new evangelists to start to explore and discern what God might already be doing in the neighborhood. Where are the needs of people in the community connecting with the grace of God to provide for relief? Where are neighbors celebrating the blessings of God, sharing their gifts with one another, and thriving in the community? These are some starting questions. They are the Luke 10 questions.

What if that same young couple, or even an individual or team, started a weekly Bible study or a monthly fellowship meal at someone's home or in some third space like a coffee shop or local pub? They would learn more and more about what God was up to in that place and how they might be called to work in service as leaders.

The compensation model could be designed to grow with the ministry. As more and more activity and responsibility occur, then more and more compensation is offered. All this should be negotiated up front as much as possible to avoid hurt feelings and miscommunications.

It seems to me that such a model allows for a much lower

risk when failure happens, and it will happen for many of the same reasons highly capitalized churches fail. It also allows for a better allocation of resources for ministry because those in charge of those resources are in touch with the needs and reality on the ground in the neighborhood.

I have heard of such ideas for starting churches but am not aware of one that is in place and working. If you are reading this and know of such an experiment and such a church plant, then give thanks to God and share it with as many others as you can. Once again, it will be in our ability to share ideas and best practices that true innovation of leadership models can occur.

It was Plato who first penned the words "necessity is the mother of invention" in his Republic. Since then, this phrase has become a proverb describing all those times when human innovation has answered the call for solutions when facing problems. The church finds itself in such a time as this.

Our leadership models need to shift and change if we are to continue to be that Jesus-filled boat, sharing the good news of God with all that gather around as in Matthew's gospel. Creativity is the key to discovering new models for ministry. Our ability to experiment with all those models, even ones that aren't necessarily part-time, will be the way to invent a future for the leadership of our church.

Creativity is Key

I invite you to take just these three models of leadership and work with them, molding and shaping them into something useful for you and your congregation or your new church plant. I invite you also to create your own models, paying close attention to God's grace and the legion of possibilities that might be found outside our traditional models of church leadership. I have invited a conversation specifically about part-time clergy, but there are other ways to consider as well. Yoked congregations in which several churches share a pastor is an old, time tested method that might be reworked for new life. My denomination is already working with non-ordained leadership models when no clergy can be found. Even congregations that donate their last remaining resources to another congregation and pastor to continue their legacy of faithfulness in the same city or neighborhood.

If Plato was right about necessity, then it's a great time to be an inventor inside the world of church leadership. Jesus said in Luke 10, *"The harvest is plentiful, but the workers are few."*[37] It's a very exciting and fruitful time again for re-imagining our models for church leadership.

---

[37] Luke 10:2 (NRSV)

11

Best Practices for Part-time ministry

"Do your best to present yourself to God as one approved by him, a worker who has no need to be ashamed, rightly explaining the word of truth."

-2 Timothy 2:15

If you read nothing else in the whole book, perhaps the church will be in a better place if a few sessions, pastors, and other church leaders read some of the hard lessons learned by those of us in full or part-time ministry. Here's a quick and unsophisticated list of some best practices:

Hiring

Attitude and intentions are everything when it comes to any job. With the right attitude, most people can learn the skills needed to be successful in the working world. If their intention is to be successful in the job they have been hired to do, it also increases the likelihood of success.

Notice I said, to be successful in the job they have been hired to do. Many times, we get tripped up when we accept a job and then immediately try and change it to another position. "I know

I was hired to do something, but I really want to do something else."

This is especially relevant, in my experience, when it comes to pastors. There is a leadership responsibility that comes with pastoral responsibilities. We are often asked to set the vision for the church. Members as well as church boards are often looking to pastors to tell them what next steps will be necessary for the church to thrive. We have already talked about how this is a dead end that doesn't lead to growth and thriving, but for the time being let's just accept the premise as operating in the work of a pastor.

Many pastors misinterpret the need of a congregation to be led with their own need to follow a job description. More simply said, sometimes pastors ignore the job description they are given and feel entitled to rewrite it to suit their own goals for ministry. Many feel they know more about what the church needs than the members or committees that might write a job description.

Best practice one: when hiring a new part-time pastor, make sure the pastor is accepting the job description you are offering and not the one they want. Sometimes pastors are really looking for full-time ministry and accept part-time as a steppingstone to get to full time. That's certainly fine if the intention of the church is to grow their pastoral leadership role into full-time. However, if the intention of the church is to stay part-time, you can see the tension that is already looming on the horizon from day one.

Pastors, make sure the church's job offering matches what you want to do in ministry. If the job requires two days a week and you only have time for Sundays, then you do yourself a disservice by accepting the position thinking the church will love you enough to accept your shortcomings when it comes to hours and time worked.

Lastly, when it comes to hiring, a great attitude on the part of those hiring and those accepting will go a long way towards success. When I first started in part-time ministry, I openly admitted to my congregation that I didn't fully know or understand how to do part-time ministry. My attitude was a willingness to learn and an openness to engage with the church as we figured it out together. The congregation also adopted an attitude of learning and openness to match mine. I believe this was the first step in successful ministry together, a matching attitude in working together.

Job Description

I have been simply amazed that more than often than not, churches do not have job descriptions for their pastors. When I was a full-time pastor, as a second career pastor coming from the business world, I had to ask that my session write a job description for what they expected from me. As stated earlier, there is a flawed idea out there that clergy already know their job and the congregation shouldn't tell them what they should do.

Of course, ministers bring certain competencies to a job and many of those are transferable from one position to another. However, every context in ministry is not the same. There are different staff needs, different programmatic schedules, and even unique requirements of the community a pastor is called to serve. So, it's necessary to write down what the congregation expects the pastor to do.

As a pastor, you should never accept a job without a job description. At first glance it might seem like it's no big deal.

The congregation trusts that you will do the job you were hired to do, faithfully and skillfully. I'm sure that's true.

The problem arises when you come to realize that you are not being evaluated on the twelve or fifteen competencies listed in a job description, but instead 40 or 400. Every member has a different idea about how you should do your job, and many times they are not the same idea. Without an agreed upon standard of measure for your success or failure, you will be at the mercy of all those expectations.

The best practice is to carefully, and with as much detail as possible, sketch out a basic job description. What are the outcomes you are expected to be responsible for? What skills and abilities will need to be deployed regularly in order to accomplish those outcomes? How often will you be evaluated to see if what you are doing matches what is expected? Who do you answer to, on an everyday basis and in evaluation form? These are just a few of the questions that should be addressed in a job description.

Writing down expectations for clarity is never a bad idea and in no way means the congregation doesn't trust the work of its pastor. It's simply a way to get everybody on the same page from the beginning to avoid misunderstandings and conflict later.

Please, please, please write down a job description for your pastor, part-time or otherwise. At the back of this book is a sample job description that might help you begin to form your own.

Compensation and Benefits

When I started in my current position, I was able to have a healthy conversation with the committee calling me to the job as well as the board approving the compensation package. Right from the beginning, we established that the compensation package was okay to talk about and even negotiate.

Yes, it's true that pastors and other church leaders are called by God to serve. It's also true that many of those same pastors have families and even if not, they have financial obligations that need to be met. It should not be an uncomfortable conversation to discuss compensation and benefits with an incoming pastor, part-time or otherwise.

Ministry jobs are a little unique when it comes to compensation and benefits. In secular jobs, often a position comes with a salary and benefit offering but most of the people in the hiring process don't know just exactly what that position costs the company doing the hiring. Instead, they have an approved number to work from. Even when it comes to increases in compensation, typically those raises are discussed as a percentage increase to existing compensation. When someone asks you what your salary is in such a secular position, it's the number on your W-2, right?

But in the church, often the compensation is discussed in terms of what it costs the church. Salary, housing allowance, medical, pension, and even professional expenses are one collective number. When pastors interview for positions, often they are given the range of compensation in terms of what it costs the church, not what they will receive on their W-2. When considering the compensation of a part-time pastor, this is the reality that must be kept in mind for both sides.

When I interviewed for my current call, I was told what the total number the church had to work with was. From there, I was invited to help consider the best way to deploy that total cost to the church in the best way for my situation. For me, healthcare was a need for my family. So, a large percentage of my total compensation goes to pay our denomination's cost for healthcare and retirement. My salary is far less than that number. I don't need other professional expenses, other than mileage, so that expense is not included. Others that have healthcare from a spouse or another position might want their compensation in a housing allowance or just as a salary. It could be that a part-time pastor's total compensation is just benefits if that's all the resources a congregation can afford. Of course, many denominational systems have minimums to consider, and even such minimums should be open to honest conversation and consideration about how they are functioning in a new part-time clergy paradigm.

I would encourage churches that are considering part-time ministry to be as flexible as possible in how compensation is put together. Determine the total number the church has to work with and invite a pastoral candidate to help allocate it in the best way for them. It shouldn't matter much to the church how that number works to the best advantage of the pastor, of course with the caveat that nothing unethical or unlawful is happening. I have even reached out to our denomination's benefit program to ask that they be more flexible in how compensation and benefits might be handled for part-time clergy denominational-wide. Such efforts are being considered.

Many industries are beginning to reevaluate their compensation and benefits program in an environment where there are too few workers for the number of jobs available. It's a competitive job market, and I believe churches should understand such a reality too. How attractive you make the compensation and benefits program will be in direct proportion to the quality of part-time pastor you retain for employment. I wonder, if the compensation for part-time clergy were more accommodating and friendly, would more pastors consider moving to such a status?

Again, the pastors I know are very conscientious men and women who do what they do because they are called by God and not because it's financially lucrative. That being said, it's still important for churches and pastors to be open and honest with one another about the financial aspect of their relationship to ensure that both sides are satisfied.

Hours

What's the definition of part-time? Is it a certain number of hours? Is it part of the full responsibility of a full-time pastor? This is another one of the questions the church is just beginning to grapple with in a new paradigm shift of church culture. How many hours should a part-time pastor work?

The first step might be to use the first few best practices in this book to design a position, complete with job description, compensation, and benefits, to determine the job that will be scheduled by hours. How long might we expect that the list of responsibilities might take a person to complete effectively, keeping in mind that often there are "other" things that can also be part of a typical work schedule? So, maybe part time is 10 hours per week or maybe three-quarter time if the congregation and responsibilities list is large enough to require that amount of work. There are at least two things to keep in mind when considering the hours of a part-time pastor.

The first is to be realistic. Many pastors, because they love what they do and are conscientious, will work more hours than they are supposed to work. I often smile when I hear my clergy colleagues say they have no idea how they could possibly do their job part-time. What most of them mean is that they feel like ministry is their whole life. It's their identity, which we dealt with in an earlier chapter. They work far more hours even than their full-time schedule allocates. They work nights and weekends and holidays. These are the pastors that do everything, often without taking any time off for vacation or study leave. As discussed, this is not a healthy model for success, for many reasons.

A best practice is to make sure what we are asking clergy to do is being done with a realistic expectation about the time it will require. If the pastor is full-time, can they regularly get the work done in 40 hours per week? Of course, there will be times when funerals or special events require a longer work week, but this should be the exception and not the rule. Part-time clergy should operate in the exact same way. If the job requires more than 20 hours per week regularly, then don't set a schedule for 20 hours a week. If it's 10 hours per week, then make sure the workload matches 10 hours per week. Everybody will soon be frustrated if we aren't clear about the hours worked compared to the job description.

Second, consider the unique nature of Sunday hours provided your church does the majority of its worship on Sunday. It's not really part-time ministry if the pastor is required or requires herself to be in the pulpit every Sunday except the 4 weeks of vacation they receive just like their full-time colleagues. Part-time ministry must mean more than just part-time office hours or pastoral care responsibility.

In the church, Sunday is sacred time and so it should be handled as such. In my current call, I have negotiated for at least one Sunday per month off. I typically work 20 hours per week. Even at one Sunday a month off, I am still working Sunday's at three fourths time. However, this affords me more of a part-time reality when it comes to the expectation for Sunday worship. It's also a way for me to maintain a healthier balance between my other commitments, real estate work and family.

Sundays off might be problematic for some congregations because the only time many members have regular interaction with the pastor is during Sunday hours. So, it might seem like the pastor is less available if they are seen less on Sunday. This might require a little education from the church board or session as to the job description of the pastor and in how the pastor spends their time other than Sunday. This is a great opportunity for the church to share more details about how their pastor functions within the leadership system of the congregation.

It's also a great way for those other than the pastor to be seen in worship. Maybe there are other part-time staff that can handle worship during the pastor's absence? What a great way to highlight the youth program or the parish associate that does visitation, by giving them a primary role for that Sunday in worship. The church will be healthier when other voices are heard and not just the "official" worship leader's.

In much the same way as compensation and benefits, best practice for hours is to be flexible and open minded when it comes to arriving at an arrangement that works effectively for everyone. Trust the pastor and the church board to come up with the right schedule to effectively accomplish the necessary tasks and be honest with one another about how it's working. If adjustments need to be made, then make them.

One last thing: I have found it effective to start with less hours at first when a new position of part-time pastor is created. It's often much easier to add hours to a schedule when things become too much than it is to find that there is not enough work for the hours allocated. It's particularly frustrating for a pastor to feel as if they don't have enough to do, and as we have discussed before, many pastors will then find other things not on their job description to do. That will hamper the ability of someone else in the congregation to realize their ministry and that's not good for anyone. Start low and work up if necessary.

Integration

The next best practice might seem like the opposite of when the pastor has too much time on their hands. What if a part-time pastor suddenly discovers they have too much to do and not enough time to get it all done? Or maybe there are those pastors or church leaders reading this and thinking, there is no way I could do another full-time job while at the same time serving a congregation as even a part-time pastor?

One of the things I discovered is the miracle of integration. In my world of real estate and ministry, as we have already discussed, there are lots of places where my so-called "careers" crossover and complement each other. We often help people I have met through my church work with real estate needs, and vice versa. At the moment of this writing, the church I am serving is in the middle of a massive multi-purpose development with new homes, condominiums, retail stores, restaurants, etc. My knowledge of real estate and development is an asset for my church work, knowing how to best position the church as a close neighbor to all this growth.

If possible, and this is better work to do on the front end before taking a position or hiring for one, try and imagine how the different parts of a work week might integrate? Are there crossover hours, in which you can be working in one place and connecting with your "other job"?

Of course, this is not meant to be dishonest or shorting either side of your obligations to employment, either the church or the other profession. However, in our world of technology and the ebbing and flowing work hours and locations, it's not that much of a stretch to be able to integrate two professions together into a workable success for all parties involved.

Evaluation

Along with job descriptions, another often overlooked part of the personnel process in many churches is regular and effective evaluations. If it's uncomfortable to write a job description for many in our congregations, then think about how difficult it is for some to see the need to evaluate the performance of the pastor against that same job description.

Here again, our lack of understanding about what a healthy evaluation represents is the reason many don't make it a priority. Whether the pastor is full-time or part-time, a regular evaluation should be conducted. An evaluation is an opportunity to communicate about what is going well and where there are areas for improvement. It's also a way to revisit the priorities of a pastor to ensure the job description has the pastor focusing on the right areas of ministry. Maybe a new ministry has emerged since the last writing of the job description. An evaluation offers a time for a personnel committee or a church board to include that in the responsibilities of their pastor. Perhaps a ministry has ended or a partnership with another organization has come to a close. The evaluation is the perfect time to adjust the job description to reflect that new reality.

I would recommend an evaluation twice a year for all employees. Many churches have a budget process that considers whether a pastor will receive an increase in salary or benefits.

The perfect time to do an evaluation is just prior to such a budget process because it will offer the finance committee the most up to date information about the effectiveness of the pastor. Who would ever want to give the pastor a raise, only to find out in the next few months in an evaluation that performance is suffering and the congregation is unhappy? It's a mixed message to the congregation when someone says, "Didn't we just give our struggling pastor a raise?"

Such an evaluation should be an examination of the performance compared to the job description. It's conducted by officially named church leaders. It should be the opinion of those leaders as to the performance of the pastor, informed by others if needed by surveys or discussions. Evaluations are not surveys filled out by the congregation and the results shared with the pastor. Evaluations should be confidential with an agreed upon written report offered to the larger leadership body or congregation. If the pastor or board cannot agree on such a written report, then the evaluation should state that such a disagreement exists and publish the results. Understand if it gets to the point in which the evaluation is conflictual, then it would serve the church well to reach out to a larger jurisdiction for mediation and support. It's important that an evaluation process be clear and transparent, especially for clergy, in a world that has seen too often abuse by clergy and a lack of trust in large church systems.

The second evaluation might be less formal, perhaps at the mid-point between yearly budget dependent evaluations. I have used such an evaluation as a check-in opportunity over coffee or lunch. It's called a mid-year evaluation, but it's more like a conversation than the formal evaluation process. It's interesting that often I have learned something about an employee during one these evaluations that would not have surfaced during a formal evaluation process.

Things like, what do you need in resources to do your job more effectively? Are you taking enough time off to recharge your batteries and sustain your ministry long term? How is your family handling the additional responsibilities or ministry obligations? When someone is being formally evaluated, they will often not be willing to share anything that might be misconstrued as a complaint or shortcoming. A mid-year evaluation is a great opportunity to see and hear different thoughts. It's not the same as the formal evaluation and is as much an opportunity to hear from the pastor as an employee as it is to evaluate performance.

If there are problems with performance that are being addressed, then the mid-year evaluation is also a great chance to check on progress towards growth and success. It's really up to the situation as to the best way to use a mid-year evaluation to be effective for the church and the pastor.

Pastors, if you are at a church without an evaluation process, then I would encourage you to insist on one. It's your chance to find out how you are doing. It should not be threatening or hostile. I always wanted to know how my ministry was being heard and seen by others. Am I hitting the marks you want me to hit or are there things I am not doing that you wish I were? It's a great opportunity to get mutual understanding on what you are doing. Don't let yourself be cheated out of an evaluation just because it's uncomfortable or something the church doesn't know how to do. Maybe your role is to model an evaluation process and demonstrate why it's important.

Lastly, I have often said that if the only time an employee of mine hears about an issue is during an evaluation, then I have not done my job as their supervisor. Yearly and even mid-year evaluations are not the time to bring out all the shortcomings of an employee that you have been saving in the desk drawer for months. Church leaders should work alongside the pastor to support them even if all the news isn't always good news. Of course, every conversation with your pastor should not be a critique or even used for constructive criticism, but if there is a problem, make sure the pastor knows about it in real time. Don't just wait for the evaluation.

Celebrations

The last best practice offered is the most important to me of all. One of the things I have discovered as I have re-entered the business world is just how badly the church does celebrations of success. It seems funny to me that an entire organization based on love and grace would find it so difficult to find time to honor and celebrate achievements.

In the real estate world, much like other kinds of sales, celebrations and awards are a regular part of the business. Each month, a list of those at the top of accomplishments are published for everyone to see and to celebrate. At the end of the year, there are annual awards banquets with trophies and medals and other kinds of recognition for a job well done. There are even small, more regular awards given for excellent customer service or encouragement of one another. It's an important part of the culture of our brand in real estate to regularly celebrate the blessings we enjoy.

How often do we take the time to celebrate and recognize our blessings in the church? Whether our pastor is part-time, full-time, or something in between, we would do well to celebrate with them regularly. Do you know how many years your pastor has served the congregation? Is there an annual celebration of her tenure? If the pastor earns another degree, is there recognition? If the community honors the pastor with a position on the board of their organization or with a community service award, does the church take time to celebrate?

The practice of celebration should not just be limited to the pastor either. Each year, those that have volunteered as Sunday school teachers and youth leaders should be celebrated. When the church does a potluck, do those that brought food to share have a way to be celebrated if with nothing else, applause? When the church does a volunteer workday on the church grounds, perhaps having each member stand and be recognized is a simple way to honor and celebrate the gifts that are being given to a congregation. It's important to the culture of a congregation.

Pastors, you set the tone in the way you handle celebrations. If you regularly thank and celebrate people in your congregation, then others will see that as the expectation and expression of the whole church. You might be surprised to see how small seeds of celebration can spill over to others. The church will celebrate you more often because you celebrate them more often.

What if we set it as a best practice, or maybe even a challenge, to find something to celebrate every month? On communion Sunday, in place of the offering, we offer a celebration of someone in our church. Or maybe during announcements on the third Sunday of every month we given someone a Trinity Award, "you and us and God" celebrating together. There are countless ways to celebrate success and blessing in ministry.

As a last best practice for celebrations, we adopt the slogan for Nike... Just Do It!

Sustainability

One of the greatest advantages of part-time ministry, in my opinion, is that it is a much more sustainable option for all involved. Churches utilizing such a model will find that they have far more resources to work with for ministry, as well as sustaining property and programs. Pastors that are part-time can live fully and successfully in two worlds, one that often feeds the other.

In my own congregation, there were many lean years with funding shortages. There are still remnants of those years all over campus. Donated furniture and half completed projects because the money ran out. Some of our technology systems and worship elements don't work quite right because they were donated or rescued from the trash pile during the years when the church had no way to purchase what it needed.

Since I arrived and the church adjusted to a part-time pastor's salary and benefits, the church has replaced the front doors, replaced the roof, put new windows in the Fellowship Hall and in the church manse. There is new carpet in the sanctuary and new choir robes being worn by the choir. During my first year, we renovated an old church library into an archives room to capture the history of our 175-year-old congregation. The manse has been renovated with new bathrooms, new floors, a new hot water heater, paint, and carpet. These are just some of the changes to the physical building, finally handling long overdue maintenance.

But the physical improvements are just part of the story. The church is dreaming again about what's possible because they have resources to work with. We have formed a new partnership with our local food bank, donating resources and time. Out of our abundance, we are giving more to local missions and even to our own presbytery. There is a feeling of gratitude because the congregation doesn't have to worry as much about the church surviving into the next generation.

The combination of an identified mission plus the freedom of new resources has transformed the congregation. There is a palpable energy when we gather that I believe will sustain this congregation long into the future.

The reality is we just can't keep doing things the way we have done them for generations, hiring full-time pastors and staff to lead our churches. The full-time model was built on disposable income and disposable time, both of which are now in short supply. The best practice of sustainability for our churches is adopting the part-time model for clergy leadership.

For the pastor, there is also sustainability in the model. It might not seem so at first. You might be wondering, how can having two jobs instead of one be more sustainable?

I believe the success of the model is located within how the pastor feels about their vocation. Pastoring churches has gotten very difficult. Our culture in North America and Europe continues to trend away from organized religious practice and the respected role that clergy had in small town America is no longer as prominent in an increasingly secular culture. As we have discussed prior, the need for congregations to see their pastors as having the answers for the future has also put a lot of pressure on our clergy. The combination of these factors makes leading churches difficult to sustain for many pastors today. I can't tell you the number of full-time pastors I know that are struggling under the weight.

The part-time model offers a pastor a chance to be outside of that world, at least for part of his or her vocation. Having another job is a respite from the ever-increasing pressure and frustration. As was discussed previously in this book, each vocation begins to inform the other. If a healthy balance can be maintained, then I believe it's a much more sustainable way to lead a church than as a full-time pastor. There will always be full-time clergy no doubt, because the needs of larger congregations will dictate the need for full-time administrators and pastors. However, I do believe pastors leading smaller churches would do well to consider the part-time model as an option.

12

Final Thoughts: Gifts of God for the People of God

"Rejoice always, pray without ceasing, give thanks in all circumstances; for this is the will of God in Christ Jesus for you."
-1 Thessalonians 5:16-18

And so, we come full circle! At the beginning of this discussion, I confessed my own sense of burnout with full-time ministry and a need to leave it behind to do something else. I remember those days of frustration and pain. Like many of my colleagues, I had a lot invested in the profession of ministry. Just the idea that all of that might be wasted and lost was almost overwhelming. How can we just walk away from our ordination vows and the call to serve God with our lives? I still wonder if this is the reason many of my friends and colleagues in ministry continue to labor daily in a job they have lost interest in and passion for?

I see them still at clergy gatherings and denominational meetings, weary and burdened by the sense of loss. "What went wrong?" is the question written all over their blank stares. Most of us, clergy or not, know the stories of pastors that succumb to addiction because of the burden they feel for their calling. There are stories of infidelity and sadly even suicide. A few years ago, a congregation I did some mission work with tragically discovered their pastor had taken his own life, scribbling a note describing his sense of loss and the burden he felt he could no longer carry. It was a devastating loss to everyone involved and one that most in the congregation did not see coming. Again, the question they uttered again and again was, "What went wrong?"

What If This Is the Spirit of God?

It's very clear to me that the church is changing, right along with the rest of culture, business, technology, entertainment, healthcare, and just about everything else. We have already talked at length about all those cultural and religious shifts. Our first reaction to change is often a negative one. We resist. Even if the change ends up being a positive outcome, much better than the old way, our first thought is usually regret. It's human nature—it always has been and likely always will be.

But there is a difference in my mind between the changes we are enduring and how we react to them. What if nothing is wrong, but instead there is a normal evolution of systems and culture? What if that evolution is not in spite of the Spirit of God, but because of it? I don't mean to suggest that God intends that we suffer because of change. But maybe it's not the change that causes us to suffer, but instead our reaction? Our expectations and our lack of adaptability might in fact be more of the reason for our suffering than anything happening externally.

Think about it this way: if it is the Spirit of God behind the changes, then do we imagine God intends that those changes cause us grief, addiction, dysfunction, or worse? Maybe there are examples from the history of God's people that might help us identify when the Spirit of God was moving in ways that nobody expected?

In the year 70 CE, the Temple in Jerusalem was destroyed. In fact, it had been a long time coming. The relationship between the Romans and the Jews living in Palestine had been tense for generations, evident in the crucifixion of our Lord Jesus. There were uprisings and revolts both before and after the life on earth of Christ. Finally, by the year 70, the Romans had had enough. They sacked and burned the entire city. The historian Josephus reported that over one million people were killed during this final battle of the Roman-Jewish war. The Temple was razed.

Now, if you were a Christian living in or near Jerusalem in the years just prior to the Temple's destruction, it had been a hard few years. It was difficult for the Jesus Way sect of Judaism to remain within Judaism. Just four years before, James the Just of Jerusalem, named as the first Bishop in Acts 15, was stoned to death by the Jewish Sanhedrin. Prophets and oracles began to warn Jewish-Christians that the leadership of Judaism was becoming more and more hostile to their belief in Jesus as Messiah. It was time to leave the great city under threat that believing in Jesus Christ could get you killed. For families that had lived and worshiped in Jerusalem for generations, it was a devastating reality to have to come to grips with.

To make matters worse, many believed that the return of Jesus was imminent and that the place of his return would be the city of Jerusalem. How could they abandon their hope in the second coming of Christ? The scriptures said that all the nations of the world would come to the city of Jerusalem to worship the true King of Kings. To leave the city now would seem to have been a betrayal to their eschatological hope in all that God was doing up to that point.

The same question would have been on the lips of these first Christians. "What went wrong?" How could this have happened to the church? Were we not faithful enough or persistent enough? Did we not suffer enough for our Lord? I imagine there was a great deal of suffering involved in the years leading up to the destruction of the Temple, the city of Jerusalem, and even more after. In fact, I am not sure our modern sensibilities can even comprehend what it must have been like to live through such times.

But what if nothing was wrong? What I mean is, what if the Spirit of God was moving in these days? Again, I don't mean in causing the suffering of men or women, faithful or not. But what if God was moving in transitioning the Christian community, even when the early Christians had no idea it was happening?

Their leaving the city prior to its destruction saved their lives. Had they still been inside as residents, would they not have joined the multitude of innocent victims that lost their lives? Maybe nothing was wrong with the faith, but instead it was adapting and changing?

In fact, one of those early persecutors of Christians in the city of Jerusalem was a man named Saul. He was feared by the early Christian community for the ferocity of his opposition to them, and the brutality in which he pursued them. And then God moved in his life, and Paul became the most effective missionary the world has likely ever known.

In the years prior to the sacking of Jerusalem, Paul was evangelizing in ways that seemed to some to be wasteful and maybe even unfaithful. Why invite the Gentiles to faith in Jesus Christ? Are they not outside the covenant in the way God intended? Paul was using his precious time and the attention his story garnered with any audience to spread the good news to what is now Greece and Turkey. But once Jerusalem was destroyed, Paul had already planted the seeds of Christian faith that would grow and eventually become the official religion of the very empire that was destroying the city most assumed to be the forever center of faith. It's an incredible historical irony.

If you had been a Jewish-Christian living in or around Jerusalem in the years prior to and after 70, you would likely have believed that something was dramatically wrong with faith in Jesus, when in fact the Spirit of God was moving and shaping Christian faith for generations to come.

It's a Very Exciting Time to be Part of Small-Church Ministry

Maybe there is a powerful lesson in this history for us. Rather than assume that the changes we are enduring with our culture and religious practice, especially as it pertains to Christian leadership, is all wrong, we could instead imagine the Spirit of God moving in us and in our churches to create something for generations to come.

Again, that's not to say that those suffering are out of touch or somehow opposed to what God is doing. However, for those of us that have seen some hope and energy in a different model for pastoral leadership, it's exciting to imagine that the Spirit of God might be behind all these days we are living through.

That same surprising evangelist Paul, when writing to the church at Thessalonica, urged his church to rejoice, to pray, and to give thanks for all the circumstances of life, because we believe that Jesus Christ is working through the Spirit of God for our blessings. God still intends good for those that trust in God's will, and so maybe our expectation might be that the days we are living through are still under God's control. If changes are to come for us and our labor of faith called pastoring, then can we bring ourselves to believe that maybe God intends that some of us serve churches in part-time ministry?

At the end of the discussion, I believe God does in fact intend that more of us serve churches in a different way. For the reasons described at length in this book, I think it's a very viable option and one that many churches could begin to consider. Not because it's a faltering from the intended better full-time model, but because it offers some benefits and gifts not possible with clergy that are limited to just one vocation. I also believe it's a very exciting time to be in small church ministry for many of the reasons cited in this discussion. Effectiveness in ministry is connected to effectiveness in other parts of our lives.

There is also innovation and energy in small church ministry that I attribute to movement by the Spirit of God. In a culture that seems to believe that only large is viable, especially when it comes to faith communities, it's a little counter-cultural to find something special in small church leadership. Given the history of our faith, in which the *"Holy Spirit blows where it wishes,"*[38] those of us blessed enough to connect with what God is doing have realized the best of our calling.

What's Your Elevator Invite?

In fact, the last thing to leave behind is what I once knew as an "elevator speech" or "grocery store" invite. When I was in sales years ago, we used to talk about encountering a client in an elevator and realizing we only had the time from when the doors closed to when they reopened again to position our product or say something of value. So, we practiced our "elevator speech."

---

[38] John 3:8 (NRSV)

The idea is a short, concise few words of meaning to describe something we wanted to share. The same is true when you meet someone in the grocery store, and again have only a few seconds to a few minutes to share something important before the ice cream starts to melt.

At the end of this discussion, what would be our "elevator speech" about the value of part-time ministry? How might we convince that haggard, tired preacher to consider lifting herself out of the mire of "what went wrong?" What could we share with a member of the church board facing not enough resources to hire a full-time replacement, as a way of encouragement and hope for an even more exciting option?

You need to write your own, but here's mine:

"It's a real gift from God to discover something unexpected and I have found that part-time ministry has connected me with what God is doing in my church and in my community in ways I would have never imagined when I was a full-time pastor. I think there will likely always be some pastors that serve in only one vocation, but the Spirit of God is opening the door of innovation and energy to more and more of us that serve in multiple ways and it's going to be a lot of fun to see where this journey with Jesus Christ and his church takes me. It sounds strange, but with less hours, I am more available to ministry than I have ever been. If you are interested in exploring this option further, I would love to share more of these gifts of God for the people of God."

13

Appendix

Can We Call You Part-Time?
Suggested Job Description

Modify and adapt this basic job description for use with your part-time pastor

Overview:
The Part-Time Pastor is primarily responsible for preaching, teaching and pastoral care, working with the leadership of the Session and in collaboration with the members of the congregation to achieve the mission of God and ministry of the congregation.

Essential Responsibilities:

- Motivate and energize the congregation, session members, and other friends of the church, seeking to ensure that the leadership and volunteers of the church have the support and resources needed to flourish in their ministry.

- Ensure that worship is well-planned, executed, and aligned with theological values shared by the members of congregation.
- Preach and administer the sacraments on a regular basis.
- Provide pastoral care for members and friends of the congregation, to ensure that every person knows their value as a child of God and minister of the gospel.
- Teach from scripture to lead the church toward discerning God's calling for its future, and inspiring members and friends to know and follow Jesus.
- Attend and moderate session meetings and nurture the leadership capacity and needs of session members.
- Inspire and participate in special events that build momentum for the church's ministry.
- Inspire and participate in formation programming (e.g., small groups, Sunday morning classes, etc.).
- Create opportunities for people seeking a church to find it and engage with the church, including leading and coordinating welcome and follow up with visitors.
- Represent the church in the community (for example, at city events where clergy presence is appropriate or requested) and in the presbytery.

Reporting Relationships:

- The part-time pastor reports to the session of of the church. The part-time pastor maintains the agreed upon _____ hours of work, reporting to the Session anytime hours are misaligned with job expectations. The part-time pastor is evaluated according to this agreed upon and published job description on a yearly basis.

Epilogue

It's Official!

Well, it's official. On a beautiful Sunday in November I was officially installed as the part-time Pastor of First Presbyterian Church of Spring Hill, TN. Friends that have been part of this journey from full-time to part-time stood with me as I again took the ordination vows, answering the constitutional questions as I have done many times before. My heart is full.

For the last three years, I served as interim pastor and the congregation and I worked hard together to figure out if a part-time model would work. It's not perfect, and it never will be. However, for the most part we are celebrating our success. As the preacher for my installation service said in his message, "Congratulations to the congregation for their courage and even willingness to try something different." The whole Christian church continues to shift and change, post pandemic, and I continue to believe it's congregations and even pastors that are willing to step outside of the norm that will partner with God for transformation. Those that go in search of what the Spirit of God might be up to will sustain and even grow their churches.

Let's count some blessings: the congregation has grown by 20% since I arrived three years ago. When a visitor attends worship in our very traditional, historic sanctuary, they can feel the energy. This is clearly a congregation that is alive and well. That's not something I did on my own, to be sure, but the empowerment by the Spirit of God of an entire group of disciples serving in ministry. People from our community are drawn to what God is doing with us.

Since my arrival, we have completed years of deferred maintenance on our campus and buildings. In the past, there was just not enough money to complete those projects and the leadership of the church had no choice but to put them off. Today, the church buildings have a new roof, the fellowship hall has new windows, the sanctuary has new carpet, the entire building has been painted and wood rot repaired, the choir have new robes, and a tired old church library has been converted to an archives room displaying historic artifacts of our 175-year-old congregation. In addition, the church manse has been renovated inside and out with a new roof, new bathrooms, new windows, carpet and paint. There are other projects such as removal of a tree that was in deteriorating condition, and improvements to our playground. At our most recent session meeting, the line item for capital maintenance was reduced in the budget because our leadership is comfortable that after three years of hard work, the property is once again in great shape. To be clear, all those projects were budgeted, planned and completed by the Session with only small help from me. I still marvel when I drive up to the church on Sunday and see another project completed, most of the time without my knowledge or approval.

Finally, and maybe most importantly for all of us, our church has renewed our commitment to serving together. The nominating committee was appointed this year and tasked, as they are every year, with nominating and electing elders for session. Never in my twenty plus years of ministry have we had church members approach the nominating committee and ask if they could serve on Session in other leadership positions. More than one person did just that, and several of them were members that rotated off while I have been moderator. They are excited about what is happening in our congregation and want to be part of the leadership again, so soon after completing their term. For the first time I can ever remember, we have too many people that want to serve and have started building a tool that will streamline and make utilizing God's blessings of volunteers in a more efficient way.

I could go on sharing the blessings God has provided in the last three years in this congregation, but instead, I'll share just one more: Like most congregations, we had to shut down during the height of Covid, making sure we kept our congregation and its members safe. Prior to the pandemic shut down, we averaged between 65 and 70 in weekly worship. That's out of just less than 100 members, which is pretty amazing already. We were closed for months and did our version of online worship, just as many other churches did. When it was time to reopen, nobody really knew what would happen. I am very happy to report that today we still worship between 65 and 70 in weekly worship. In fact, it's really more than that and we are very grateful. I know many churches have struggled with reopening, and this is not to say that we don't grieve with those that continue to struggle, but we also celebrate our community.

Just in case you think I am just a full-time pastor in part-time pastor's robes, let me also say just a couple words about my full-time job. The Middle TN area has exploded and our real estate team has been busy helping our clients find homes. Our team has had the best three years we have ever had, building year upon year. We hired a full time operations manager who has done an amazing job with managing our ever-growing client base. Finally, we have hired and fully on boarded two additional agents to help us meet the demand. The relationships we enjoy with our clients and our team are an everyday blessing Paula and I don't take lightly. We are counting those blessings, not just in the innovations of my church work, but also in the way of life they provide for my family.

If any of this sounds like bragging, it isn't meant to—it is merely our joy and enthusiasm for what we see God doing here. This congregation of God's people did take a risk along with me in hiring a part-time pastor, who still has no intention of ever working full-time again. It's been quite a time of experimenting and learning together these last three years. What I love most is when I hear members of the congregation repeating the joy they feel about what has happened. It's infectious and most certainly the presence of the Spirit of God. My family also regularly celebrates the difference part-time ministry has made for us in the time we spend together.

What I still find most profound about this journey is how much I enjoy being somebody's pastor again. Of course, everything can and might come apart in the next three years, and I have also learned that's okay. Sometimes the Spirit of God is moving and shaping our lives when we don't realize it. My hope is that we continue to innovate our leadership and our lives to partner with God in transforming not only the church, but the world around us too. Thanks be to God!

About the Author

The Rev. Dr. Chris Adams was a full-time PCUSA pastor for over twenty years before stepping away from full-time church leadership as a real estate entrepreneur and part-time pastor. His doctoral work was completed at Fuller Theological Seminary with an emphasis on missional ministry. Chris has years of experience in business, leading and administrating churches, and working with not for profits, large and small. His daily focus is helping develop Christian leadership that can innovate and thrive in today's ever changing church and business culture. He and wife Paula own and operate the We Live Here TN Team at Keller Williams Realty in Franklin, Tennessee, exploring ways for life and faith to intersect through community development and everyday relationships. Chris loves spending time with family, mountain biking, and having fun at the beach.

You can connect with me on:
- https://callyouparttime.com
- https://twitter.com/revdrchrisadams
- https://www.facebook.com/callyouparttime